Illustrated Handbook
of Vernacular Architecture

Illustrated Handbook of

VERNACULAR ARCHITECTURE

R. W. Brunskill

faber and faber
LONDON · BOSTON

First published in 1971
by Faber and Faber Limited
3 Queen Square London WC1N 3AU
Second edition, 1978
Third edition, revised
and expanded, 1987
Reprinted 1988

Printed and bound in Great Britain by
Redwood Burn Limited
Trowbridge Wiltshire
All rights reserved

© *R. W. Brunskill 1971, 1978, 1987*

British Library Cataloguing in Publication Data

Brunskill, R. W.
Illustrated book of vernacular
architecture.—3rd ed.
1. Vernacular architecture—Great Britain
I. Title
720′.941   NA961
ISBN 0–571–13916–7

Library of Congress Cataloging-in-Publication Data

Brunskill, R. W.
Illustrated handbook of vernacular architecture.

Bibliography:p.
Includes index.
1. Vernacular architecture—Great Britain
2. Architecture, Domestic—Great Britain.
3. Farm buildings—Great Britain. I. Title.
NA7328.B83   1987   728′.0942   86-11560
ISBN 0–571–13916–7 (pbk.)

CONTENTS

List of Illustrations   *page* 9

Preface and Acknowledgements   15

Preface to Second Edition   17

Preface to Third Edition   17

Introduction   18

1. Walling: construction and materials   34

2. Roofing: shape, construction and materials   72

3. Plan and section   98

4. Architectural details   122

5. Farm buildings   142

6. Urban vernacular and minor industrial buildings   164

7. Comparisons and conclusion   184

Appendix 1: How to study vernacular architecture, extensive, intensive and documentary   214

Appendix 2: Glossary notes   228

Notes, References and Recommendations for Further Reading   232

Index   250

ILLUSTRATIONS

INTRODUCTION

1. Domestic, Agricultural and Industrial Vernacular *page*
   (M.U.S.A.) 21
2. Distinction between size-types (RWB) 23
3. Diagrams illustrating the vernacular zone (RWB) 29
4. Initial example, Fan-isaf, Merthyr Cynog,
   Brecons. (R. E. Williams) 33

WALLING: CONSTRUCTION AND MATERIALS

5. Stone, irregular types: Cumrew, Cumb. (RWB) 37
6. Stone, irregular types, diagrams (RWB) 39
7. Stone, regular types: Cumwhitton, Cumb. (RWB) 40
8. Stone, regular types, diagrams (RWB) 41
9a. Cobbles: Keswick, Cumb. (RWB) 42
9b. Pebbles: Norfolk (M.U.S.A., D. P. Housego) 42
10. Cobbles and Pebbles, diagrams (RWB) 43
11. Flint: Dorset (RWB) 44
12. Flint, diagrams (RWB) 45
13. Brick: Louth, Lincs. (M.U.S.A., R. Hallam) 46
14. Brick, diagrams (RWB) 47
15. Brick (continued): Ipswich, Suffolk (NMR) 48
16. Brick, further diagrams (RWB) 49
17. Earth, clay, cob, etc.: Stanwix, Cumb. (RWB) 50
18. Earth, clay, cob, etc., diagrams (RWB) 51
19. Timber frame walling: Ticehurst, Sussex (RWB) 52
20a. Cruck-frame: Herefords. (RWB) 54
20b. Box-frame: Essex (M.U.S.A., R. A. Cordingley) 54
21. Cruck-and-box frame construction, diagrams
    (RWB) 55
22. Timber walling, jettied construction: Weobley,
    Herefords. (RWB) 56
23. Timber wall construction, diagrams (RWB) 57
24. Wattle and daub infill: Leominster, Herefords.
    (RWB) 58
25. Wattle and daub infill, diagrams (RWB) 59
26. Plain tile hanging: Kent (RWB) 60

27. Plain tile hanging, diagrams (RWB) *page* 61
28. Mathematical tile hanging: Kent (M.U.S.A.,
    R. A. Cordingley) 62
29. Mathematical tile hanging, diagrams (RWB) 63
30. Weatherboarding: Dedham, Essex (M.U.S.A., D.
    P. Housego) 64
31. Weatherboarding, diagrams (RWB) 65
32. Plaster Cladding: Colchester, Essex (M.U.S.A.,
    R. A. Cordingley) 66
33. Plaster Cladding, diagrams (RWB) 67
34. Other cladding materials: Devon (RWB) 68
35. Other cladding materials, diagrams (RWB) 69
36. Brick nogging: Dorset (M.U.S.A., M. A. Taylor) 70
37. Brick nogging, diagrams (RWB) 71

ROOFING: SHAPE, CONSTRUCTION AND
  MATERIALS

38. Roof construction (M.U.S.A., R. A. Cordingley) 72
39. Roof shape, chimneys and dormers: Dedham,
    Essex (M.U.S.A., D. P. Housego) 74
40. Roof shape, hipped roof family, diagrams (RWB) 74
41. Roof shape, gabled roof family, diagrams (RWB) 75
42. Single and double rafter roofs (M.U.S.A.) 76
43. Single and double rafter roofs, diagrams (RWB) 77
44. Aisled barn: Coggeshall, Essex (NMR) 78
45. Aisled buildings, etc., diagrams (RWB) 79
46. Butt purlin roofs (M.U.S.A., R. A. Cordingley) 80
47. Butt purlin roofs, diagrams (RWB) 81
48. Through purlin roofs (RWB) 82
49. Through purlin roofs, diagrams (RWB) 83
50. Thatch: Dedham, Essex (M.U.S.A., A. M.
    Horner) 84
51. Thatch, diagrams (RWB) 85
52. Slate: Denton, Cumb. (RWB) 86
53. Slate, diagrams (RWB) 87
54. Stone flags: Gt. Orton, Cumb. (RWB) 88
55. Stone flags and stone tiles, diagrams (RWB) 89
56. Plain tiles: Dedham, Essex (M.U.S.A., D. P.
    Housego) 90
57. Plain tiles, diagrams (RWB) 91
58. Single lap tiles (pantiles): Westow, Yorks. (RWB) 92

59. Single lap tiles, diagrams (RWB)   *page* 93
60. Chimneys: Sussex (RWB)   94
61. Chimneys, diagrams (RWB)   95
62. Dormers: Abingdon, Berks. (RWB)   96
63. Dormers, diagrams (RWB)   97

PLAN AND SECTION
64. Plan forms, the first floor family: Neadon, Devon,
    (RWB)   100
65. Plan forms, the first floor family, diagrams (RWB)   101
66. Plan forms, the open hall family: Dorset
    (M.U.S.A., M. A. Taylor)   102
67. Plan forms, the open hall family, diagrams (RWB)   103
68. Plan forms, the two-unit family: Cumb. (RWB)   104
69. Plan forms, the two-unit family, diagrams (RWB)   105
70. Plan forms, the central fireplaces family: Essex
    (M.U.S.A., D. P. Housego)   106
71. Plan forms, the central fireplaces family, diagrams
    (RWB)   107
72. Plan forms, the inside cross-passage family: near
    Brecon (RWB)   108
73. Plan forms, the inside cross-passage family,
    diagrams (RWB)   109
74. Plan forms, side-wall fireplace family: near Exeter
    (RWB)   110
75. Plan forms, side-wall fireplace family, diagrams
    (RWB)   111
76. Plan forms, the double pile family: Cumb. (RWB)   112
77. Plan forms, the double pile family, diagrams
    (RWB)   113
78. Sectional form (M.U.S.A., J. A. Drabble)   114
79. Open Hall types, diagrams (RWB)   115
80. One and a half storey types, diagrams (RWB)   116
81. Multi-storey types, diagrams (RWB)   117
82. Inserted fireplace, Charlwood, Surrey (RWB)   118
83. Hearths, smoke-bays, fireplaces, diagrams (RWB)   119
84. Staircases, diagrams (RWB)   121

ARCHITECTURAL DETAILS
85. Architectural details: Colchester, Essex
    (M.U.S.A., R. A. Cordingley)   122

86. Windows, the medieval phase: Crickhowell, *page*
    Brecon (RWB)   126
87. Windows, the medieval phase, diagrams (RWB)   127
88. Windows, the sub-medieval phase: Sebergham,
    Cumb. (RWB)   128
89. Windows, the sub-medieval phase, diagrams
    (RWB)   129
90. Windows, the renaissance phase: Louth, Lincs.
    (M.U.S.A., R. Hallam)   130
91. Windows, the renaissance phase, diagrams
    (RWB)   131
92. Doorways, the medieval phase: Lavenham,
    Suffolk (M.U.S.A., P. B. Lockwood)   132
93. Doorways, the medieval phase, diagrams (RWB)   133
94. Doorways, the sub-medieval phase: Lessonhall,
    Cumb. (RWB)   134
95. Doorways, the sub-medieval phase, diagrams
    (RWB)   135
96. Doorways, the renaissance phase: Thurstonfield,
    Cumb. (RWB)   136
97. Doorways, the renaissance phase: diagrams
    (RWB)   137
98. Other external ornament: Colchester, Essex
    (M.U.S.A., R. A. Cordingley)   138
99. Other external ornaments, diagrams (RWB)   139
100. Internal ornament (RWB)   140
101. Internal ornament, diagrams (RWB)   141

FARM BUILDINGS
102. Location and layout, typical farmstead: Cwm-du,
    Brecons. (RWB)   146
103. Location and layout, diagrams (RWB)   147
104. Combination arrangement: Cartmel, Lancs.
    (RWB)   148
105. Combination arrangements, diagrams (RWB)   149
106. The barn for hand threshing: Crickhowell,
    Brecons. (RWB)   150
107. The barn for hand threshing, diagrams (RWB)   151
108. The barn for machine threshing: Angrouse,
    Cornwall (RWB)   152
109. The barn for machine threshing, diagrams (RWB)   153

110. The cow-house Llangasty tal-y-llyn, Brecons. *page*
(R. E. Williams) 154
111. The cow-house, diagrams (RWB) 155
112. The stable: Talgarth, Brecons. (R. E. Williams) 156
113. The stable, diagram (RWB) 157
114. The granary/cartshed: Hay, Brecons. (R. W.
Williams) 158
115. The granary/cartshed, diagrams (RWB) 159
116. The shelter shed and the linhay, diagrams (RWB) 160
117. The hay barn and the field barn, diagrams (RWB) 161
118. The pig-sty, and the dovecot, diagrams (RWB) 162
119. The kiln and the oast house, diagrams (RWB) 163

URBAN VERNACULAR AND MINOR INDUSTRIAL
BUILDINGS

120a. Urban vernacular before the Industrial
Revolution: Louth, Lincs. (M.U.S.A.,
R. Hallam) 165
120b. Urban vernacular after the Industrial Revolution:
Hyde, Cheshire (M.U.S.A., R. Tilley) 165
121a. Medieval urban vernacular: Colchester, Essex
(M.U.S.A., R. A. Cordingley) 166
121b. Medieval urban vernacular, diagrams (RWB) 167
122. Urban vernacular, late 17C., York (RWB) 168
123. Urban vernacular, 16C. and 17C.: diagrams
(RWB) 169
124. Urban vernacular 18C. and 19C.: Rye, Sussex
(M.U.S.A., J. P. Griffiths) 170
125. Urban vernacular 18C. and 19C., diagrams (RWB) 171
126. Early cottage industry: Haskayne, Lancs (RWB) 172
127. Early cottage industry, diagrams (RWB) 173
128. Later cottage industry: Langley, Cheshire (RWB) 174
129. Later cottage industry, diagrams (RWB) 175
130. Early industrial houses, diagrams (RWB) 177
131. Later industrial houses: Rochdale, Lancs. (RWB) 178
132. Later industrial houses, diagrams (RWB) 179
133. Windmills and watermills: Nether Alderley,
Cheshire (RWB) 180
134. Windmills and watermills, diagrams (RWB) 181
135. Bottle kiln (Gladstone Pottery Museum) 182
136. Smithies, kilns, etc., diagrams (RWB) 183

COMPARISONS AND CONCLUSIONS

137. Walling and roofing materials: The Solway Plain *page*
     (RWB)   184
138. Map of building regions (RWB after P. Smith)   185
139. Map of stone walling (RWB)   187
140. Map of flint, pebbles and cobble walling (RWB)   188
141. Map of brick walling (RWB)   189
142. Map of clay, etc, walling (RWB)   190
143. Cruck-frame distribution (RWB)   191
144. Timber frame walling distribution (RWB)   192
145. Map of cladding materials (RWB)   193
146. Map of thatched roofing   194
147. Map of stone flag and stone tile roof covering
     (RWB)   195
148. Map of plain tile and pantile roof covering (RWB)   196
149. Map of fireplaces, with cross-passage and in front
     side wall (RWB)   197
150. Map of fireplaces in central position (RWB)   198
151. Some time scales (RWB)   199
152. Vernacular architecture in North America—
     Harper's Ferry, VA (RWB)   200
153. Early American vernacular, northern:
     Portsmouth, New Hampshire (RWB)   202
154. Early American vernacular, northern, diagrams
     (RWB)   203
155. Early American vernacular, southern: Ocean
     Hall, Maryland (with later verandah) (RWB)   204
156. Early American vernacular, southern, diagrams
     (RWB)   205
157. Dean's House, Dunblane, Perthshire (RWB)   206
158. House at Lewiston, Inverness-shire (RWB)   208
159. Scottish vernacular, diagrams (RWB)   209
160. Vernacular Revival: Wilmslow, Cheshire (RWB)   210
161. Vernacular Revival: House at Rochdale by Edgar
     Wood, diagrams (J. H. G. Archer)   213
162. Typical record cards (C. Woodhead and RWB)   217
163. Simplified recording questionnaire 1. (RWB)   218
164. Simplified recording questionnaire 2. (RWB)   219
165. Measured drawing example (M.U.S.A., M. Purdy)   223
166. Inventory example (RWB)   227
167. Concluding example (RWB)   231

NOTE. Items marked M.U.S.A. are from the collections of the
Manchester University School of Architecture.

Preface and Acknowledgements

Like so many of my age-group (the young middle-aged) I am only one generation removed from the land. I have therefore had the privilege, which may not be available to my own children, of spending school holidays on the farms of my grandparents, uncles, and cousins and taking part in a way of life which, as recently as thirty years ago, retained intact many of the traditions accumulated over several centuries. It was during such holidays spent in remote parts of Cumberland and Westmorland that I first became aware of differences of walling material, roofing material, plan form and architectural detail, and it was from practical if inexpert activities that I began to realize the significance in different forms of farmstead layout and farm building design.

As a student at the School of Architecture in the University of Manchester my interest was detected by Professor R. A. Cordingley, encouraged and guided until I was ready to participate in the postgraduate study of vernacular architecture which he had initiated in the late 1940's. I played my part between interruptions of military and professional activity in the extension of the study during the following decade, building on the experience of my predecessors and helping to develop techniques which have been adopted by succeeding graduate students. We had all assumed that, on his retirement in 1963, Professor Cordingley would draw together our various regional studies and use them as the basis for a comprehensive and authoritative account of vernacular architecture in England. His sudden and untimely death within a few months of retirement cruelly shattered that assumption.

However, it had become apparent that interest in vernacular architecture had been growing simultaneously and independently in other, and perhaps more appropriate centres than Manchester, and in 1954 the Vernacular Architecture Group had been founded to bring together in an informal study group the widely scattered and diverse interests of architects, archaeologists, historians and museum curators. The rapid growth in the numbers and authority of the Group showed that there was a wide general interest in the subject and a largely untapped enthusiasm for the study of the surviving buildings of a rapidly changing rural economy. With this in mind I began to adapt the rather ambitious objects and somewhat elaborate techniques of Professor Cordingley's study to the more limited objectives and lesser capabilities of architectural

15

students. With the encouragement of Professor N. L. Hanson, this was done and seemed successful. I then began to make the further adaptation needed to extend the study amongst members of archaeological societies and extra-mural classes who had no architectural training but considerable enthusiasm. This further adaptation included the publication by the Ancient Monuments Society of the 'Systematic Procedure for Recording English Vernacular Architecture', and, from this, there developed the suggestion that some simple handbook might be produced which would amplify the basic information collected through completing record cards and would also assist in full understanding of the accounts of vernacular architecture based mainly on documentary sources which were now becoming available. The preparation of this handbook was the result.

Although I have taken most of the photographs and prepared all the diagrams specifically for this book, and must take responsibility for the facts recorded and opinions expressed, its preparation would have been quite impossible without the published work noted in the list of references and recommended for further reading. The help of my colleagues in the University of Manchester, especially Dr. Wood-Jones and Dr. Marsden, is gratefully acknowledged, and my former colleague, J. H. G. Archer, was kind enough to approve my comments on the Vernacular Revival and allow me to use his photograph of the Edgar Wood drawings. The discussions during many conferences of the Vernacular Architecture Group have opened my eyes to many unfamiliar parts of the country and sharpened my understanding of what I had thought familiar; special mention must be made of the following who have helped on specific points: Dr. P. Eden, Dr. E. Gee, R. A. Foster, Sir Robert Hall, T. M. Owen, S. R. Jones, E. Mercer, Miss V. Parker, Dr. J. E. C. Peters, P. Smith, J. T. Smith, and W. J. Smith. I must thank students of the School of Architecture for the drawings and photographs which have been adapted and Professor Hanson for permission to make use of them. Some of the sections include information gained with the benefit of the Neale Bursary and a Research Grant of the R.I.B.A., and, in the case of American material, as one of the by-products of a Commonwealth Fund Fellowship of the Harkness Fund and a Staff Travel Grant of Manchester University. I must also thank the Breconshire Education Committee and Deiniol Williams, their Chief Education Officer, for the opportunity to conduct research into farm buildings in the county. The students at the Vernacular Architecture Summer Schools which I have conducted for several years as part of the programme of the Institute of Advanced Architectural Studies, University of York, have been willing guinea pigs for recording techniques, and sharp critics of my theories, and I am grateful to them and to Professor P. Nuttgens for this opportunity.

Finally I must thank my wife for typing the draft manuscripts and Mrs. Johnson and Miss Beck for the final typing; and also Mr. Peter Crawley and his colleagues for humouring an architect who insisted on trying to design a book rather than write it.

Wilmslow, Cheshire, February 1969   R. W. BRUNSKILL

Preface to Second Edition

It is now almost ten years since work began on the *Illustrated Handbook of Vernacular Architecture* and nine years since the bulk of the text was completed. The subject of vernacular architecture has attracted a great deal of interest and much enthusiastic support over this period and I have tried to incorporate in this revised and enlarged edition a small part at least of the large amount of new material which has emerged and has been published. Additions have been made to nearly all sections of the book but the sections on house plans, both rural and urban, have been very considerably extended. The American pages have been altered to bring them more closely to English precedent. Major additions have been made to the Notes and References section in order to help the reader dip into the much enlarged pool of published material on vernacular architecture.

I am grateful to the reviewers who have made helpful comments and to the many readers who have written to me with comments, corrections and additional pieces of information.

The traditional counties and imperial measure are retained.

Wilmslow, Cheshire, September 1977   R. W. BRUNSKILL

Preface to Third Edition

Since the publication of the second edition progress in the study of vernacular architecture has continued apace as I have attempted to acknowledge in this third edition. The Notes and References section has been completely rewritten, a brief introduction to the vernacular architecture of Scotland has been added, some maps and diagrams have been added, redrawn or extended, and minor corrections have been made.

Once again I am grateful to reviewers and correspondents for helpful comments, fellow-members of the Vernacular Architecture Group for discussion and to my wife and daughters for their continued forbearance.

Wilmslow, Cheshire, December 1985   R. W. BRUNSKILL

INTRODUCTION

Forty years ago, the serious study of vernacular architecture in Great Britain had scarcely begun. True, three of the pioneering studies, Addy's *Evolution of the English House*, Innocent's account of *The Development of English Building Construction*, and Peate's *The Welsh House*, had long been completed, and certainly many books describing in a general way the characteristics of selected farm-houses and cottages had been published. But the careful investigation of individual buildings and the classification of comparable examples which has now made the subject such a hive of academic industry is a pursuit which has only just reached its maturity.

During the past forty years or so the study of vernacular architecture has engaged the interest of scholars in many fields and each one has contributed the techniques of his discipline to the general inquiry. Among the foremost have been the social and economic historians, looking to the buildings of the countryside to help describe the activities they were designed to house, and relating periods of intense building activity to the opportunities for the accumulation of capital. The new topographers, seeking to find the historical explanation for the intricately organized landscape of the British countryside, have related rural buildings to their wider setting. The medieval archaeologists have discovered in the study of roof construction in vernacular buildings a rich field for investigation and comparison. The Royal Commissions on Historical Monuments have, during the past three decades, turned an increasing proportion of their resources to the study of vernacular architecture. Geographers, in the transformation of their own subject, have seen in vernacular architecture evidence of the significance of quite localized geographical factors in the development of the different regions of the country. Sociologists, in their intensive surveys of individual communities, have discovered that the buildings of the people and the way they were erected, ranked with their churches and forms of religious observance in expressing their social organization. The students of folk life, in their allied field, have shown, for instance, how often architectural details and building practices have perpetuated customs whose origins were thought lost, and whose technical basis had long been transformed. Vernacular architecture has been seen as one of the ways in which regional and national character survived the various political amalgamations which make up the present nation. And to end a list which could most probably be extended, the architectural historians have recently devoted some of their attentions to the study of the many minor architectural monuments, the houses of the

18

people, the barns of their crops, and the factories of their early industrial efforts, which their brothers in practice are now so rapidly replacing.

Following on the increasing academic interest in the subject of vernacular architecture there has been an increasing public interest. This has taken the form of individual interest expressed, for instance, in the current enthusiasm for converting cottages for weekend use, as well as in the protests at planning proposals which threaten the quality of village life. It has included group interest, particularly on the part of the WEA classes who are making systematic studies of their own villages. It is now taking on a national scale in the development of environmental studies in the schools, for the study of vernacular architecture is being recognized as a major part of the study of both the urban and rural environment.

Official interest in vernacular architecture has also developed through the building conservation movement. The recently expanded lists of buildings of special architectural and historical interest include many examples of vernacular architecture while most conservation areas consist mainly of vernacular buildings. Among large landowners the National Trust has begun a survey of its vernacular building stock.

As a consequence of the academic work carried out during the past forty years there has been a respectable trickle of books and articles on vernacular architecture which can provide background reading and specific information to feed the popular interest in the subject. But a need has been established for a handbook to provide basic information on the buildings and for use in the field, and the present work is intended to go some way to filling that need. Its pretensions are modest; it will contain little that is new to the established workers in the subject, it certainly is not intended to anticipate the definitive work which the study has now justified, but if it helps the enthusiastic amateur to increase his own awareness of vernacular architecture and encourages him to add his own contribution to the national stock of knowledge of the subject, then its preparation has been worth while.

Types of Vernacular Architecture

Examples of vernacular architecture may be broadly divided into domestic, agricultural, and industrial categories. Some other building types provide examples which have been described as vernacular, for instance the small, simple churches of poor and remote parishes, or simple defensive forts or refuges not intended for permanent human occupation, or the less pretentious examples of railway and canal architecture: canal keepers' cottages, wayside halts etc. But, since the majority of examples of these other building types were professionally designed and relatively sophisticated, it seems better to confine the study to the three categories of domestic, agricultural, and industrial.

Domestic vernacular architecture comprises the buildings designed for living as normally understood: eating, sitting, sleeping, storage, etc., and also the ancillary buildings which, at certain times, have been quite extensive: brew-house, bake-house, kitchen, sculleries, wash-house, etc. The category includes defensive dwellings in the sense of private houses adapted for occasional defence, as distinct from castles which included some domestic accommodation. It also includes inns, shops, etc., where the domestic activities predominated over the commercial. A distinction is made between the domestic vernacular of the countryside and that of the towns, the one being related mainly to farming and the other mainly to commerce, and both governed until quite recently by the separate lines of development followed by town and country.

The vernacular architecture of agriculture comprises all the buildings of the farmstead apart from the farm-house and its domestic ancillaries. Thus the barn, cow-house, stable, granary, cart shed, shelter shed, pig-sty, etc., would be examples of agricultural architecture, normally in the vernacular range. The isolated field barns and out-farms and the agricultural ancillaries within a village, such as the pound, are also included.

Industrial vernacular is a term intended to include the buildings which housed industrial activities related to the countryside—wind and water-mills, corn and lime kilns, smithies and potteries, etc.—and those manufacturing activities which were related to domestic rather than commercial scale—workshops attached to dwellings or incorporated within them, and the small textile mills based on hand or water power, for example. During the Industrial Revolution, the scale of operations or the unprecedented nature of the processes took the buildings out of the vernacular class, though most operations can be traced to their domestic origin.

Size-Types

Before examining an example of domestic vernacular architecture, it is important to try to establish its size-type. Four such categories have been generally accepted: the Great House, the Large House, the Small House and the Cottage, and they correspond to four groups of householders ranging from the top to the bottom of a scale combining wealth and social status. Just as there are graduations within the scale at any period of time, so the boundaries between size-types cannot be precisely determined but the division into four categories has been found to be reasonable in application and convenient in the field.

The Great Houses were occupied by people of national importance. The great residential castles of the Middle Ages, the elaborate mansions and palaces of the 16C. and 17C., the imposing country seats of the 18C., the swollen villas of the 19C., were all Great Houses and were the homes of royalty, the nobility of Church and State, those who occupied high and profitable office at home and abroad, the landowners rich in land through inheritance or trade, the cotton barons, the railway magnates. These people were of national importance through high social status or great wealth, and occupied Great Houses appropriate to their position in society. Such houses are normally excluded from the ranks of vernacular architecture.

People of some local importance lived in Large Houses. The manor house commanding, in partnership with the church, the medieval village street, the house of the unusually successful yeoman, or the highly favoured parson, the small country house of the squire, the imposing farm-house of the wealthy tenant farmer, the house of the clothier or mill-owner, all were Large Houses, and, until the approach of the 19C. normally had qualities which make them a part of the body of vernacular architecture.

For the human backbone of the nation there were the Small Houses. The ordinary yeoman or tenant farmer, the miller, the smith, the minor official, the unfavoured parson, the shopkeeper, the schoolteacher, were people of significance in the village, but of little standing in national or even provincial society. They lived in Small Houses, and their dwellings make up the main body of material which is recognized as domestic vernacular architecture.

But at the bottom of the social scale and only just above the subsistence level were the labourers and artisans who had no wealth apart from the strength of their limbs or the skill of their hands, and the widows and

elderly whose survival depended on the charity of family or community. Undoubtedly many of these lived in the houses of their employers, patrons, or relatives, but many had simple dwellings of their own—the Cottages which eventually were built of materials permanent enough to survive as examples of the most basic domestic vernacular architecture.

The size-type given to an example of vernacular architecture—Large House, Small House, or Cottage—is decided by reference to the sort of person for whom the house was originally intended. The actual buildings tend to pass down the social scale during their lifetime; the manor house becomes a farm-house, then is divided into cottages and finally, abandoned as a dwelling, becomes a farm building or workshop.

The size-type is also decided by reference to regional conditions at a particular time. The Large House of someone of considerable local importance in a poor region might be little bigger than the Small House of a yeoman in a more prosperous region: the armigerous Welshman having a house rather less ostentatious than a contemporary Sussex farmer. Less obviously, the briefly prosperous handloom weaver of early 19C. Lancashire had a cottage which was bigger and better built than that of the depressed agricultural labourer in Norfolk at the same time.

Size-types of a sort were also found among farm buildings. Barns had high status and were given due architectural distinction and constructional thought while at the same time the young cattle, the pigs and the poultry might have scarcely any shelter at all. Even among industrial buildings some, such as the windmills and watermills housed processes so important that they were properly built from an early date whereas others, such as the drying sheds in a brickyard, rarely enjoyed the status of permanent buildings.

As in so many aspects of vernacular architecture, a distinction should be made between town and country. The grades of wealth and status in the towns were no doubt reflected in the houses, but the reflection was not a mirror of that in the rural areas.

The Vernacular Zone

From the various origins of the students of the subject there has come a variety of opinions on what constitutes vernacular architecture and which periods and which examples provide the most fruitful study. For some the medieval manor house is most significant, for others the yeoman's farm-house, the weaver's cottage, the squatter's cabin, or even the non-domestic buildings of the farm-house or the factory complex. An attempt is made here to comprehend these varying interests by suggesting a vernacular zone in which examples may be found between the period in which they appear as buildings in relatively permanent materials and the period in which they cease to have the qualities we call vernacular. Where nothing survives of the buildings, study will depend on archaeological methods beyond the scope of this book; where the surviving buildings have more than vernacular quality they may be studied by the ordinary techniques of architectural history.

The polite threshold
It has been assumed for the purpose of this study that the designers of the various buildings have made some attempt, however untutored and how-ever unsuccessful, to make the buildings pleasant to look upon—to make them, in fact, to however slight a degree, examples of architecture rather than building. Many readers will think this rather a wild assumption, but experience does suggest that the designers organized their building elements to produce more than a solely utilitarian result and with far from accidental effects.

Assuming, then, that we are considering architecture rather than mere building, another distinction is made between polite and vernacular architecture. The difference between the two is a matter of degree. The ultimate in polite architecture will have been designed by a professional architect or one who acted as such though under some other title, such as surveyor or master mason; it will have been designed to follow a national or even an international fashion, style, or set of conventions, towards an aesthetically satisfying result; and aesthetic considerations will have dominated the designer's thought rather than functional demands. Aesthetically and, probably, constructionally the designer will have been adventurous, exploring new ways of achieving his conscious wishes; in so doing his materials will have been chosen to help achieve the aesthetic or constructional ends and have been obtained from whatever source could supply such materials. On the other hand, the ultimate in vernacular architecture will have been designed by an amateur, probably the occupier of the intended building, and one without any training in design; he will have been guided by a series of conventions built up in his locality, paying little attention to what may be fashionable on an international scale. The function of his building would be the dominant factor, aesthetic considerations, though present to some small degree, being quite minimal; tradition would guide constructional as well as aesthetic choice, and local materials would be used as a matter of course, other materials being chosen and imported quite exceptionally. Between the extremes of the wholly vernacular and the completely polite, examples occur which have some vernacular and some polite content. Thus even the most sophisticated design in a provincial town may be carried out entirely in local materials and so include some slight vernacular quality, but a rough distinction can in practice be made between those buildings which have vernacular or polite qualities to a greater or lesser degree. If they are more polite than vernacular they are assumed to have passed over the polite threshold, out of the vernacular zone.

The date at which the polite threshold may be set varies with time and size-type. The very earliest examples, even of Great Houses, had mainly vernacular qualities, but most medieval buildings of this size-type were polite rather than vernacular. The Large Houses from the end of the 17C. onwards tended to be designed by architects in the prevailing style and thus moved further and further into the zone of polite architecture. Towards the end of the 18C. and during the 19C. the larger farm-houses were designed by professional designers for effect rather than utility. Even Cottages during the second half of the 19C. came to follow national rules rather than local traditions. Nowadays virtually every house bears the mark of polite architecture and has lost all significant vernacular quality. Thus the polite threshold may be indicated on a graph by a line falling at a steeper and steeper curve down the scale of size-types in approaching the effective end of vernacular architecture.

The vernacular threshold

If in England and Wales, as in the Isle of Man, it had been considered unlucky to demolish a house, we might have surviving examples of all types of house from the earliest times of settlement to the present day. Even without such a helpful tradition one would expect some examples from every period to have escaped demolition so as to give a continuous series diminishing in numbers from the present day back to the most distant past. But in fact when recording the examples of the domestic vernacular of the countryside (the situation is rather different in the towns), one finds that the many surviving buildings provide a continuous thread until a point in time when suddenly all evidence in the form of surviving buildings comes to a stop. This point varies with size-type, but it is so sudden that clearly the emergence, or complete reconstruction of houses in materials permanent enough to survive, is something of great significance. This line on a graph of size-type and time is called here the vernacular threshold. In any locality it tends to curve with an ever increasing gradient; examples high on the social scale surviving from an early period, from the middle of the social scale being more recent and from the bottom of the social scale being more recent still. Or, to put it another way, we can see examples of the vernacular dwellings of medieval knights but generally not of medieval farmers; of 17C. yeomen but not their cottager neighbours; but of 19C. artisans at the humblest level.

Modifications of the vernacular threshold
The absence of examples below the vernacular threshold may indicate either that houses were deliberately destroyed or that they were of such flimsy materials that they were not expected to survive. The strong evidence for the Great Rebuilding, which occurred throughout most of England between 1570 and 1640, explains the deliberate destruction of older sub-standard houses, most being completely replaced even though some were incorporated in improved structures. But it also suggests that for the first time large sections of the rural community had the means available for the erection of relatively expensive buildings of permanent materials and the security of tenure which would make such investment worth while. But the period of Great Rebuilding varied with location as well as social status; it occurred between about 1670 and 1720 in the northern counties of England, and later still in part of Wales, so that any average, national, vernacular threshold requires modification in any specific locality. Furthermore, the later the period of rebuilding, the more likely that it would extend far down the social scale, so that farm-houses and even cottages of medieval date have been identified in advanced parts of England whereas such houses suddenly appear together at quite a late date in more backward parts.

It is interesting that the position of the threshold does not seem to vary with the durability of the available building materials. The hardest stone of Cornwall and Cumberland is associated with a late period for the threshold, the perishable timber of Kent and Sussex may be seen in houses dating from medieval to late 19C., while vulnerable clay and cob continued in use well into the 19C. in parts of the country which were not very far distant from sources of superior building material.

27

For agricultural and industrial vernacular buildings similar thresholds could be distinguished if only dating criteria were better established for these building types. But it seems that most surviving farm buildings of brick and stone on large, medium and small farms are no older than the 17C. and few built of timber seem to be more than a century older. Those which are clearly ancient are the huge barns of the rich landowners, clerical and lay.

The vernacular zone
If one accepts the two thresholds, the one representing the extent of conscious architectural effort and the other the sudden emergence of building intentionally in permanent materials, they may be combined to form a vernacular zone. For any size-type this is the period between the emergence of houses in permanent materials but vernacular content, and the abandonment of vernacular design in favour of polite; for any period it represents those size-types for which vernacular examples survive as against those which survive but with the qualities of polite architecture. In fact the size-types and periods within the vernacular zone—medieval manor houses, 17C. yeoman houses, 18C. farm-houses and 19C. cottages —are just those which have already gained the interest of vernacular scholars and for which further field work is likely to be profitable. Beyond one extreme of the vernacular zone architectural history takes over; beyond the other extreme field investigation is a matter of archaeology.

a. the 'polite' threshold
b. the 'vernacular' threshold

c. modification of the vernacular threshold between areas of survival from early periods and areas of late survival
d. vernacular threshold of farm buildings showing survival of tithe barns from early but superior farmsteads and late construction of farm buildings at lower levels
e. modification of vernacular threshold as a result of archaeological or documentary research illuminating a period from which no complete buildings survive
f. . the 'vernacular zone' between the the two thresholds with date and assumed size-type of one hundred published dated examples of vernacular architecture superimposed

THE 'POLITE' THRESHOLD

THE 'VERNACULAR' THRESHOLD

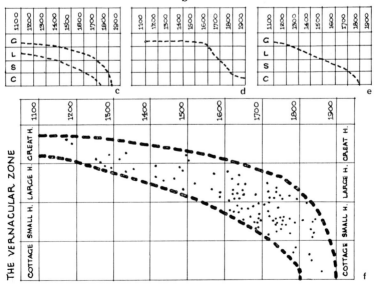

29

The Organization of the Book

This book has been prepared in order to help those who have little or no previous knowledge of the subject to an understanding and appreciation of the wealth of vernacular architecture in this country. As a handbook it is intended primarily for use in the field as a complement to the several excellent accounts of vernacular architecture, based regionally or nationally, which are now available. It has therefore been designed as a series of opposite pages, one with a photograph and short text on some aspect of the subject and the other with diagrams and explanations of what may be seen in the field. Both text and illustrations are mere tokens of what is already known of the various aspects of vernacular architecture. They may be expanded by reference to the books and articles listed in the notes and bibliography, they should be expanded by further field work, they may well be superseded as research proceeds.

The first five chapters refer mainly to domestic vernacular architecture, though many of the materials and techniques illustrated apply equally to the vernacular of other building types. They are based on the domestic vernacular of the countryside, although much of the comment could be applied to urban vernacular, and they follow the sequence most often adopted in the study of actual examples, both extensively in field surveys and intensively in measured drawing.

Walling materials are divided in the first chapter between mass construction of stone, brick, earth, or combinations and variations of these materials, and frame construction based on timber. Frame construction is further divided between half timber work with exposed framing members and infill panels of wattle and daub or brick, and the various cladding materials, tile, plaster, etc., which have been used to conceal the frame. In the second chapter, roofing problems are shown to vary according to the constructional system adopted, the roofing shape—chosen according to plan shape, sectional form, or the dictates of fashion—and roofing materials, chosen, mainly, according to local availability. In this chapter the projections from the roof—chimneys and dormers—are briefly noted. A chapter on plan and sectional form takes one into the house but also shows how the internal arrangements of these simple buildings are often revealed on the exterior. In spite of the pitfalls which hamper classification, some simple groupings have been suggested and there is a note on the developments in the design of staircases as multi-storey construction became normal even at the lower social levels. Then a chapter on architectural details—windows, doors, external and internal ornament—

shows how vernacular designs were enlivened by decoration, crude and old fashioned though it so often might be. Some general indications of place and time for the various characteristics have been given.

The next chapter extends the study to the buildings of the farmstead. The domestic vernacular of the countryside was, of course, only one component in the range of buildings which formed the setting for the intricately organized but traditionally-based society of the countryside, and recently some attention has been paid to the range of other buildings which made up the farmstead. In this chapter they have been considered as separate building types and no separate mention has been made of walling, roofing, and architectural detail which usually followed domestic precedent.

A further chapter combines some brief comments on urban vernacular and minor industrial vernacular which eventually coalesced in the terraces of industrial workers' houses which represented the last trace of vernacular architecture and which marked the change from a rural to an urban economy. The domestic vernacular of the towns has suffered more than that of the countryside from the alterations and extensions of the 19C. and it has been comparatively little studied, but redevelopment is revealing many unsuspected remains and the conservation movement is emphasizing their significance so that the balance is being redressed. The effects of early industrial developments on house design, few at first but considerable later, are now being recognized and some examples are illustrated. The developments in design of workers' houses have been ignored as long as we have been obsessed by their ugliness or their lack of those amenities which we now, a hundred years later, consider essential, but now that they are so rapidly being demolished it is suggested that they be recorded before they are forgotten.

In the concluding chapter, some attempt is made to give comparative material in the form of distribution maps and time scales. This is no more than an attempt, for too little information is at present available on a national basis, and while a good deal of material has become available for various regions the lack of standardized procedure means that comparisons cannot be carried very far. The great intricacy of the many factors which have affected vernacular architecture in this country makes the presentation of comparative material as difficult as it is important. A note on American Vernacular may remind the British reader that for a short time some of our vernacular regions were to be found across the Atlantic, and it may inform the American reader of the considerable work which has been done on this side since his standard works were written. Finally, a brief reference to the Vernacular Revival in British domestic architecture around the turn of the 19C. acknowledges the significance of this thread, and, therefore, indirectly, the whole pattern of vernacular architecture in the development of the Modern Movement.

Recent developments in the study of vernacular architecture in Scotland are acknowledged through a note on regional characteristics of this part of Britain.

Appendices suggest three ways in which the further study of vernacular architecture may be conducted. The subject is too extensive, and the rate at which examples are disappearing too rapid, for the very few professionals to cope alone. Most of our information on vernacular architecture has been collected, analysed, compared, and published by amateurs, spending leisure hours in furthering their own understanding of the countryside in which they lived and worked. This little handbook serves only to extend and assist the greater numbers who are now so desperately needed.

Initial Example

This suggests items to be observed in sequence in analysing an example of vernacular architecture.

(*Opposite*)
a. walling material, shape, coursing, jointing, finish
b. roofing shape
c. detail at verge
d. detail at eaves
e. material, method of laying
f. ridge
g. chimney position
h. water tabling, etc.
i. dormers, position, shape, roofing, walling material
j. plan form
k. sectional form
l. staircase provision
m. window shape
n. window frames
o. door shape
p. door details
q. relationship between farm buildings and farm-house
r. use of farm buildings.

1. WALLING: CONSTRUCTION AND MATERIALS

GENERAL

More than any other single component, the choice of walling material establishes the character of an example of vernacular architecture. It is the wide range of walling materials available and the intricacy of their distribution which gives the unique variety to vernacular construction in England and Wales.

With choice of walling material there is related the choice of structural system, though, as we shall see, the two are not necessarily directly related. Broadly speaking there were two structural systems available to the designer: mass construction and frame construction. In the former, the loads of roof and floors were carried to foundations by means of walls which also provided the weather protective envelope to the activities carried on within the building. In the latter, the loads of roof and floors were carried by a frame which concentrated these loads until they were redistributed by the foundation; the weather protective envelope was non-loadbearing (though it might carry its own weight), and could be independent of the frame (though sometimes it filled spaces between the members of the frame). Both mass walling and frame construction have been used at one time or another over virtually the whole country and, even at the present day, it is not certain that one or the other has become the inevitable choice in domestic construction.

Materials used for mass construction included stone, flint, cobble, brick and earth. Of these, only earth produces a homogeneous mass; all the others are jointed and rely on the skill with which the individual pieces have been put together, and the suitability of the jointing material as well as the quality of the basic material, for stability and weather excluding properties. The succeeding pages examine briefly the characteristics of walling employing these various materials.

The material used for frame construction was almost invariably timber; there are very few examples in which iron has been used in vernacular building. Timber frame construction may follow the box-frame or the cruck-frame schools of carpentry, and the problems of distinction between these two schools will be noted. Buildings of box-frame construction may have panels of wattle and daub, exposing the structural and non-structural timber, or the frame may be entirely concealed behind a cladding of plain tiles, mathematical tiles, weatherboard, or lath and plaster; alternatively the panel may be brick filled. Buildings of cruck-

34

frame construction may have timber framed walls—in which case they are difficult to distinguish externally from box-framed buildings—or they may have walls of some material normally associated with mass construction: stone, brick, flint, cobble, or earth, when they would outwardly be indistinguishable from buildings entirely of mass construction.

As a rule, the walling materials used in vernacular construction were exposed in their natural state, but for reasons of weather protection or fashion they were often concealed. Thus, both wattle and daub panels, lath and plaster cladding and earthen walls were lime-washed, and poor quality masonry was often rendered and lime-washed, while, especially during the early 19C., buildings of any material might be stuccoed and painted in order to meet the demands of the prevailing architectural fashions.

WALLING MATERIALS—mass walling

Setting aside for a moment earthen construction, which presented its own special difficulties, the problem of achieving stability in walls made of separate pieces of materials—stone or brick—was one which must have been ever-present in the minds of the vernacular builders, and governed to a large extent their techniques of construction.

Stability of foundations was not usually a serious matter for the quite small low buildings erected by mass constructional methods, but as an aid to foundational stability as well, perhaps, as a survival from a previous form of construction, the use of large rounded boulders, especially in areas of morainic deposit, was common at the base of mass walled buildings.

Collapse by outward buckling of the walls in section was avoided with the aid of heavy floor beams which tied opposite walls together, and this may be one reason why such heavy beams were used. Outward pressure on the top of the wall was countered by the use of heavy tie beams, self-balancing roof members triangulated to transmit loads vertically down the walls, or by transferring roof loads as far down the wall as possible.

There was an equal danger of collapse by outward buckling of the wall on plan. This was countered by introducing cross walls to help divide a long narrow plan into squarish self-buttressing cells and, sometimes, by the use of horizontal timbers bonded into the coursing of the walls as reinforcement. Where brick walling succeeded timber framing this particular danger was not always recognized, and, having the benefit neither of the interaction of a framed structure nor the internal buttressing of a properly organized mass construction, brick walls either bellied out or were tied back with the aid of iron rods and plates.

35

The strength of a mass-constructed wall being reduced by every opening, there was a limit to the number, size and proportions of window openings. This was in contrast to frame construction where, in theory, every panel could be as conveniently transparent as opaque. Normally, therefore, window openings in mass walls were few and narrow. But where good quality stone, confident masons, and architectural fashion came together, long tall ranges of mullioned and transomed windows might be displayed.

However adequate the general precautions against collapse, the strength of a mass wall depended on the concerted action of its individual members. Good quality stone, which falls naturally into block shapes, presented fewest problems, and walls of, say, millstone grit, permian sandstone or oolitic limestone could be comparatively slender in section. Poorer quality stone, such as clunch, would need reinforcement by use of dressings or lacing courses of better quality material. Large stones, such as Cornish granite, presented such problems in bonding and jointing that a thick wall was unavoidable. Small rounded stones such as cobbles, pebbles and flints were so difficult to bond satisfactorily that they were bedded in deep clay and held together with the aid of frequent horizontal lacing courses and reinforced quoins and jambs. Even if bonding problems could be overcome there was the problem of jointing to be solved. Compact or irregular stones required thick joints and, until lime for mortar became cheap and plentiful, these joints were made simply of earth or clay. In extreme examples one might wonder whether a wall was made of cobbles bedded in earth or of earth mixed with cobbles, or indeed whether a stone wall had been laid with dry joints or whether leaching of clay had led to an effect of dry walling.

Monolithic earthen walls presented their own problems of stability and erection, and generally low height, wide walls, small cubic compartments, and narrow openings are characteristic of this form of mass construction.

Stone: Irregular Types

The following notes refer to walls of the tough, irregular masonry most commonly found in vernacular construction.

At the base of a wall the heaviest stones were used, and these were often boulders of such enormous size that one wonders how they were manoeuvred by hand into position. It seems likely that in many cases these stones acted originally as a plinth to walls of timber or clay and may have survived more than one reconstruction of a building. The main wall would be composed of undressed field stones, quarry faced stones, or straight cut stones, in each case obtained from the ground close by the building under erection. The walls were usually rather less than two feet thick and depended on the bond obtained by overlapping the tails of pieces of irregular depth which backed into the wall from its surfaces; bonding or 'through' stones were placed at intervals to run right through the wall, though in parts of the Northern Pennines they projected beyond the wall face as a series of ledges. The interior of the wall was normally packed with small loose pieces of waste stone. Joints were usually made as horizontal as the nature of the stone permitted, though a 'watershot' technique, in which stones were bedded to slope towards the outer face of the wall, may be found in the Lake District. A somewhat similar technique is found in the Pennines, especially on the western slopes, where the surface is composed of receding facets of each stone, rather like weatherboarding upside down. Drystone walling, in which no bedding or pointing material is used, was very rarely used in buildings, though normal for stone field walls.

While the local stone was used for wall construction as a matter of course, superior stone or brick was often used for bonding purposes, as lacing courses at intervals up the wall, for quoins, and as dressings to doors and windows. Such superior material might be carried for several miles across geological boundaries. Even in the general walling, more than one type of stone might be used if locally available, and sometimes bizarre polychromatic effects were the result.

In many parts of the country, irregular stones were bedded in clay, as revealed when walls of such material fall into ruin. Sometimes the clay was leached away by rain water penetrating the outer skin of the wall even to such an extent that the construction appears to be that of drystone walling. Where available at reasonable cost lime mortar was used for bedding. Such mortar was locally made of limestone or chalk or sea shells crushed and burnt to produce quicklime which was taken, carefully protected from damp or rain water, to the building site where it was slaked and in due course mixed with sand to produce the mortar. Whatever the bedding or jointing mortar, rubble walls were pointed with lime mortar wherever feasible. The pointing was usually finished flush with the surface of the stone; projecting ribbon mortar as often seen in restoration work is not traditional.

(*Opposite*)

SHAPE: Much of the character of a stone wall comes from the shape of the individual pieces of which it is composed. Thus one may contrast the compact, irregular types e.g. (*a*) Kentish Rag, the elongated irregular types e.g. (*b*) Mountain Limestone, the hard, thin, slaty types e.g. (*c*) Lake District Slate, and the quarry faced millstone grit blocks (*d*) of the Yorkshire Pennines, as well as many others.

COURSING: Irregular 'rubble' may be built entirely uncoursed (*e*) i.e. without any continuous horizontal joints; built to courses, (g) i.e. brought to a level joint at regular vertical intervals; snecked, (f) i.e. with a regular joint interrupted at intervals; or coursed, (h) i.e. with every horizontal joint continuous.

QUOINS: During the erection process, careful attention was paid to the corners of a building which may be raised by a more skilled craftsman, the general walling between being done by the less skilled. In most masonry techniques the cornerstones, or quoins, are bigger and better finished than the rest, (i) and may be further emphasized (j).

JOINTING: Irregular stones have wide joints which have originally or later been so pointed with lime mortar as to spread over the surface of the wall (k). Sometimes little stones were pushed into the joints as 'galletting' (l). Where a bedding material was unprotected by pointing it would be leached away by rain water to give the effect of a 'dry joint' (m).

RENDERING: To give weather protection or as an improvement to inferior stone, lime-sand rendering was sometimes used (n). This was trowelled to a rough surface or was dashed with pebbles, or was whitewashed. In some districts whitewash applied directly to the stone built up year by year to give an effect of rendering (o).

Stone: Regular Types

Although the vast majority of stone-walled vernacular buildings are clearly made of different sorts of rubble, the use of ashlar was not unknown at the vernacular level, and tended to develop from the use of squared coursed rubble for the superior parts of a building.

In ashlar work, regularity and high quality of finish are characteristic, and, where the designers of vernacular buildings wished to present a show to the world, the ashlar might well be used for the front wall of a house. But such a show was confined to the surface. The ashlar itself was backed by rubble or brick, and the end walls, even when exposed to public view, were nearly always in an inferior technique, either rubble masonry or brick. The rear wall of a house was always in the the poorest material, and showed the crudest technique of building construction.

As well as in coursing, jointing and selection of stones, ashlar masonry was distinguished by the degree of surface dressing given by the mason in contrast to the natural or crudely hammered surface to rubble used by the waller. The use of mason's tools in vernacular work has not been properly investigated as yet, but it seems plain that the drafted margins, picked, combed, and rubbed work of superior masons were adopted, after an appropriate time lag, at the humbler levels.

Even where the main body of the wall was in rubble, dressed stone was often used for the significant parts of a wall. In millstone grit, red sandstone, and oolitic limestone districts especially, dressings, worked sometimes to a fine finish, were quite normal even in vernacular buildings.

SHAPE: Stone being a natural rather than an artificial material even the ashlar work of vernacular building involved irregularities. Where each course was of uniform height the stones would vary in length (*a*), and both length of stone and height of course could vary without substantially affecting the richness of appearance (*b*).

COURSING: Ashlar work was normally coursed, though snecked walling could be of ashlar quality. Sometimes courses were of an even height but more often they varied in height in such a way as to diminish towards the top of the wall (*c*).

Ashlar dressings to a rubble wall gave a key to the coursing (*d*).

QUOINS ETC.: As the individual pieces of ashlar masonry were carefully squared it was not always considered necessary to take extra precautions at the corners (*e*). However quoins were stressed where the general walling was of small stones or where architectural fashion demanded. Projections, plinths and string courses were used for similar reasons (*f*).

JOINTING: Fine jointing was customary in ashlar work (*g*), even though the ashlar surface was bonded into a more crudely jointed rubble backing (*h*).

FINISHES: Stucco, a fine smooth faced plaster, was the ashlar equivalent to rendering on rubble masonry. It was, of course, applied to inferior stone, but the intended effect was presumably that of ashlar and, indeed, imitation joint lines were sometimes incised (*i*). Dressings were modelled in stucco or were in superior masonry with stucco applied to the general wall surface (*j*).

Cobbles and Pebbles

The following notes refer to the use of cobbles—rounded stones picked from river beds or fields on the Boulder Clay—and pebbles—small rounded stones, sea-worn, and picked up from the shore. Techniques of use are generally similar to those of unworked flint, though the geological origin of the material is quite different.

Both cobbles and pebbles can only be used for building purposes with great difficulty. Cobbled walls are often rendered and whitewashed so as to be almost indistinguishable from similarly finished walls of stone or clay. Pebbled walls, composed of a material so tiny in scale but deep in texture, give quite exotic effects. In both cases some other material is necessary for dressings to door and window, and desirable at the corners.

Both materials tend to be seen on late and humble examples of vernacular building, but cobbled walls were often used at the side and rear of buildings in which the front wall was of brick or unpainted stone, while pebbled walls may be found as an affectation giving character to a cottage ornée.

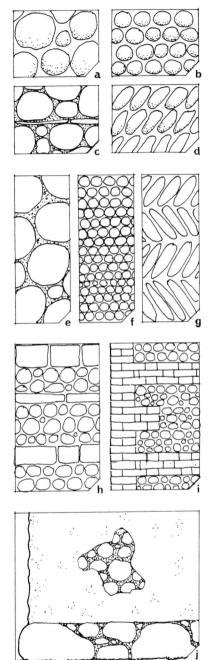

SHAPE: Essentially rounded, the material having been worn by ice action, by water action in the upper reaches of rivers or by sea and tidal action on beaches, including the inland remainders of former beaches. Pebbles are usually less than 3 ins. in diameter (*b*), cobbles between about 3 ins. and 9 ins. in diameter (*a*). Generally the materials are globular but they may be flattened (*c*) and egg-shaped (*d*).

COURSING AND JOINTING: Cobbles were often laid uncoursed, relying on clay bedding to maintain stability (*e*). Pebbles, being more uniform in size, were usually laid in courses (*f*). Elongated pebbles or cobbles may be laid in diagonal or chevron pattern (*g*).

REINFORCEMENT: Surviving examples of both cobble and pebble walling tend to be late, and reinforcement at quoins, jambs, and by lacing courses will usually be found to be of brick (*i*). However, cobbles are also found with bands of other stones and walls may be laid in alternate courses of cobble and stone (*h*).

RENDERING, ETC.: Because of the poor appearance of a cobbled wall, and the difficulty in preventing loss of the jointing material, rendering is quite common (*j*). Seashore pebbles, both on the Sussex and the Norfolk coast, have been tarred as a weather protective measure. The irregular surface modelling and the soft corners of unreinforced cobbles or pebbles help to distinguish such walls when rendered.

43

Walling Materials: Flint

Flints are irregularly shaped nodules of silica, found in gravel beds, usually from the upper and middle layers of chalk formations. Like pebbles and cobbles they can only be used with great difficulty for building purposes but, nevertheless, in the absence of other walling materials, they have been quite widely used in South and East England.

Taken straight from the ground, the egg-shaped flints were laid precariously in courses, the outer surface of the wall being brought to a reasonably fair face by plentiful use of mortar and with galletting of small chips of flint set in the joints, the inner ends of the flints being allowed to tail into the wall. More commonly the flints were split to give a fairly flat outer surface to the wall, though still with side joints. Split flints could be further chipped to give a flat, square end, usually about four inches across. In both cases the broken surface of the flint, initially black, developed a white 'rind'.

Although flint can be used without reinforcement to a considerable height—as church towers, both round and square, in East Anglia will bear witness—the material is not really suitable for square corners, e.g. for door and window jambs in small scale vernacular building, and it is most commonly found reinforced with other building materials.

Many people find flint used alone rather drab, but when used in combination with other materials the effect may be highly decorative. At a superior level, as in the well-known Gatehouse of St. Osyth's Priory, Essex, the combination of flint and limestone can be quite spectacular, but even in humble work, the stripes and chequer patterns of flint, brick, and limestone are quite fascinating.

SHAPE: The flints used in walling are rather like a series of flat-topped teeth, each with a root tailing into the wall (*a*). In ordinary flint walling, the exposed ends are round and irregular on surface, in knapped flint work they are square and smooth surfaced (*b*).

JOINTING: This varies between ordinary and knapped flint work. In both varieties the flints are laid in courses, but in the former there are wide joints between the rounded flints (*c*), whereas in the latter, joints are thin, forming a fine net effect over the black wall surface (*d*).

REINFORCEMENT: To help form square corners, brick or stone was used at quoins and at the jambs of door and window. These reinforcing materials were block bonded into the flint (*e*). Horizontal lacing courses of brick or stone ran right through the flint walls at a vertical interval varying from about one to three feet (*e* and *f*).

PATTERN: As well as the overall pattern of flint and joint, and the emphasis given by dressings and lacing courses, a chequer board pattern of alternate panels of stone and flint may sometimes be seen (*h*). In superior work a tracery of thin limestone was combined with the flint (*g*).

Brick Walling

Bricks had been used in the Eastern Counties as a walling material for superior buildings during the Middle Ages, but came into use for vernacular buildings during the periods of Great Rebuilding in the 16C. and 17C. The use of brick spread throughout the areas formerly dominated by timber frame construction and, in spite of the Brick Taxes which were applied with varying degrees of severity from 1784 until 1850, brick had become the universal building material in England and Wales by the second half of the 19C.

The use of bricks had become fashionable in polite architecture towards the end of the 17C. and this undoubtedly helped to popularize the material at the vernacular level. As well as encouraging new construction in brickwork, fashion led to the use of bricks as false fronts or in total encasement of timber framed buildings. The disastrous fires in towns and villages, culminating in the Great Fire of London, gave a further impetus to the use of this fire-resistant material.

A further advantage of brickwork over other forms of wall construction was the way in which decorative effects could be obtained comparatively cheaply. These included surface patterns, from the use of differently coloured bricks, and surface modelling, as in the imitation of classical details and string courses in brickwork. Moulded bricks and terra-cotta came into use during the 18C. while skilled craftsmen cut, carved, and rubbed bricks to produce delicately modelled forms.

Where stone traditions were strong, bricks were used only for general walling, the dressings to quoins, windows and doors being of masonry. During the first half of the 19C. when exposed brickwork had become less fashionable, the use of stucco in general imitation of stone meant that the decorative qualities of bricks were temporarily neglected. Nevertheless, in the period immediately before the general eclipse of vernacular architecture, brickwork enjoyed a renaissance which has left many charming examples of this building material to be enjoyed.

SHAPE: Brickwork shows some variation in size and proportion when used in vernacular buildings. Early and inferior bricks were irregular in shape and size. Even after length and breadth had become standardized (*a*) height varied to reach a maximum during the Brick Tax period and again in the Midlands and North during the 19C. (*b*).

BONDING: Early and inferior brickwork showed no recognizable bond (*c*). Then English Bond (*d*) included variations in which one course of headers matched three or five courses of stretchers (*g*). The later and more decorative Flemish Bond (*e*) was modified to three or five stretchers to each header (*h*). Occasionally header bond (*f*), with each brick exposing its head, was used for display.

JOINTING: As in masonry the more irregular the material the thicker the joint. Thus, early, roughly shaped bricks required wide joints whereas the precise, machine made bricks of the 19C. showed very thin joints (*j*). As a decoration, tuck pointing gave the illusion of fine joints to coarse brickwork (*k*).

PATTERN: Different brick earths and different degrees of firing produced decorative effects. Among the most popular was the use of headers, vitrified by special firing to a metallic purple colour to form chequerboard, geometrical, diaper, or lettered pattern (*l* and *m*).

MOULDED AND GAUGED WORK: Bricks were moulded to crude classical forms (*n*) but the skilful bricklayer preferred rubbed and gauged work (*o*).

47

Brick Walling (continued)

BRICKWORK ECONOMY

The period of the Brick Taxes coincided with a wave of cottage building and various bonds were used which economized in bricks through the formation of a sort of cavity wall. The most common was Rat Trap Bond, which was like Flemish Bond except that the bricks were laid on edge rather than on bed. A wall 9 ins. thick had a cavity 3 ins. wide between outer and inner leaves of brickwork, each 3 ins. thick. Fewer bricks were needed than in a solid wall of similar height; stability was adequate for the relatively low walls and minimal loads of a cottage; some benefit in heat insulation may have been obtained; but as the cavity was bridged by each header the walls were just as vulnerable to rising damp and driving rain as solid 9 inch walls.

BRICKWORK OPENINGS

The problem of spanning door and window openings exercised the bricklayer as well as the mason and solutions were generally similar except that the standard-sized bricks made arches of large radius fairly easy to construct. The simplest and crudest was the rough brick segmental arch in which the bricks were uncut and the taper was confined to the joints. Segmental arches of rubbed or purpose-made voussoirs were also fairly easy to produce. The cambered arch which was curved at the bottom but flat at the top required much more skill and usually involved rubbed and gauged work with special bricks of a different colour from those of the main wall. Alternatively, in many vernacular buildings, windows and door openings had no outer arch or lintel, the wall being carried over a stout window frame.

48

The skilled bricklayer working on polite architecture could perform the wonders of his craft but at the vernacular level quite simple devices were effective enough.

BRICK TIES

It is clear from bulging or leaning walls in old brick buildings that some bricklayers were not clear on the need for adequate buttressing of external walls by internal partitions, and tie rods were often used in order to keep the most vulnerable parts of brick walls in position. Tie rods usually ran from gable to gable and when tightened held the walls against wrought-iron tie plates.

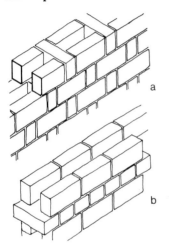

a. Rat Trap Bond showing outer and inner leaves of bricks laid on edge and with cavity in between. The header bricks, also laid on edge, run right through the wall and bond the two leaves together. *b.* Dearne's Bond: a variation of English Bond in which the stretcher courses are laid on edge, producing a cavity and economizing in bricks. *c.* Rough brick segmental arch with tapered mortar joints. *d.* Segmental arch of tapered bricks; a timber lintel behind would carry most of the loads on the wall. *e.* Cambered arch of rubbed bricks. *f.* Opening spanned by a wooden lintel.

g. Soldier 'arch' of bricks on edge: a crude device in which the bricks carry little of the load on the wall. *h.* Soldier arch of bricks on end: rather less crude and gaining some structural benefit from the friction of bricks and their joints. *i.* Dentilation in which header bricks project about 2 ins. *j.* Dog-tooth brickwork: bricks laid diagonally and projecting to carry brick courses above. *k.* Four examples of tie plates such as may be seen on the gables of brick buildings. The S shape was sometimes given the head and tail of a snake.

Walling Materials: Earth, Clay, etc.

The use of turf, clay, mud, cob, wychert, and other earthen materials available on the surface of a building site was formerly a good deal more widespread than is sometimes imagined, while the evidence of place and occupation names suggests that the practice may well have been even more widespread than surviving examples would indicate—by the nature of the material, archaeological evidence is likely to be scarce.

Materials and processes of erection varied with locality, but all gave walls which were capable, on proper consolidation, of supporting the loads imposed by vernacular buildings. However, a cruck-frame was usually used with the quick process. The following techniques may be distinguished:—

1. *Sods or turf*—surface close cropped, sods cut two to six inches depth, three feet by two feet size, laid in courses on plinth of stones, single storey height, sometimes loose stones on top to take roof timbers. Reinforcement of timber posts at corners, and along walls, sometimes those related to roof construction. Finish by paring with hay knife.

2. *Clay and straw mix, used without moulds*—clay, incorporating pebbles, chalk, etc., as available locally was moistened, mixed with chopped straw, and kneaded to a glue-like consistency. Walls were raised by either (a) *slow process*; (an interval between each lift) or (b) *quick process* (a wall of thin courses raised in one operation).

3. *Earth or clay used with moulds*—timber or wattle shuttering filled either with (a) loose dry earth, poured and rammed, or (b) wet clay.

4. *Clay blocks* (cf. adobe)—large blocks of clay (e.g. 6 ins. by 18 ins. by 9 ins.) were moulded, left to dry naturally, then laid with clay mortar. At first sight it is difficult to distinguish earth-walled buildings from those built of other materials and then rendered or whitewashed.

SODS OR TURF: There is little trace of this technique in England or Wales, though it was formerly widespread in parts of Scotland and Ireland. Walls were thick, irregular, and required protection unless used for purely temporary shelters (a).

SLOW PROCESS: Where the weather-protective coating of plaster has fallen away the joint lines between each 'lift' can clearly be seen. Usually the earth includes plenty of pebbles and chopped straw was used as horizontal reinforcement and to reduce cracking on drying out. The diagram (b) shows a boulder plinth and straw used as a thin layer between each lift as well as mixed with the clay.

QUICK PROCESS: This is distinguished by the use of thin layers of clay-like material interspersed with straw. Although originally laid horizontally the layers have usually drooped and deformed on drying out (c).

CLAY LUMP: This technique has not been widely used in England and Wales, though examples survive in parts of Norfolk, Suffolk, and Cambridgeshire. The blocks were bonded and laid in courses exactly like bricks even though considerably larger in size (d).

51

Timber Frame Walling

There are three main types of timber-based wall construction which have been commonly used in Europe: horizontal log, in which the wall was composed of solid timbers laid one on top of the other and jointed at the corners; post and plank, in which the wall consisted of a series of heavy planks slotted between even heavier posts; and timber frame, in which the structural frame was separate from the weather protective part of the wall. As far as is known, there are no examples of the first two techniques in Great Britain.

The structural distinction between cruck- and box-frame timber construction has already been mentioned; in the former, roof loads were transmitted by means of inclined crucks to the ground, in the latter they were taken on framed walls. The existence of hybrid forms of construction, and the problems which arise when a timber roof is carried on a wall of some other material, tend to obscure detailed differences in the technique, but for most purposes the difference is clear enough.

It appears that the process of erection was radically different in the two versions of timber frame. In cruck construction the A-frames were assembled on the ground, then 'reared' one by one into a vertical position so that the ridge purlin, side purlins, and wall plates could be dropped into their sockets, and tie the frames together. In box-frame construction it appears that in most cases the posts were erected separately, being propped into position either by temporary stays or by permanent diagonal braces; next, the wall plates were dropped onto the top of each post, and finally the tie beam was dropped into position, simultaneously locking post and wall plates. The intermediate studs were placed piece by piece at the same time. There were some variations in this practice as, for instance, where a 'bent' of posts and tie beams was reared, cruck fashion, or where a whole wall was framed on the ground and then reared, but these were not common.

As an aid to indentification of joints, carpenters' marks were used. These appear to have varied with time and place, but were based either on a series of Roman numerals made with a chisel, or a series of symbols made with a gouge and scratched with the point of a chisel. Sometimes all the joints on each truss were separately marked; alternatively each joint was given a number in sequence from one end of the building to the other. Presumably, both types of marking related to the erection process.

Oak was the timber predominantly used for structural purposes, though elm and imported softwoods came into increasing use. There was a general tendency to use lighter timbers as carpentry techniques improved and supplies of suitable timber diminished. In the cruck-frame tradition, this led to the use of very poor and spindly members, especially in remote areas where cruck trusses were ancillary to other load bearing construction. In the box-frame tradition, technical improvement led to the eventual elimination of the distinction between load bearing posts and non-load bearing studs so that a whole wall of members of approximately the same section acted as one. This development appears to have occurred first in the use of trussed partitions and party walls, but later spread to the external walls of small buildings. The availability of softwood timber, in uniform sections, and cheap machine-made nails meant that the elaborate joints of earlier timber framing techniques were no longer required. Two variations, platform framing and balloon framing, came into universal use in North America in the second half of the 19C., but platform framing, at least, remains in common use in this country for humble buildings such as garages and garden sheds.

One problem in the study of timber frame construction is the re-use of timber. Redundant joints and peg holes, often useful as a guide to lost members, may equally often refer to former use of a piece of timber in quite a different structural context.

Cruck-Truss and Box-Frame Construction

The distinction between cruck- and box-frame construction is not universally accepted, and the essential characteristics of cruck construction, its geographical spread, and the social status of this carpentry technique give cause for argument amongst the scholars of vernacular architecture. The problems are most acute in the cruck variants like the base-cruck (which seems like a pair of posts inclined at the top to take a collar), and the jointed cruck in which vertical post and inclined blade were joined together, sometimes with very little curve on post or blade.

Although they differ in detail, distribution maps of surviving cruck trusses show that the technique is not found in East or South East England but is normal in Central and Northern England and most of Wales. If jointed crucks are excluded, then the West of England and the south-western counties of Wales are also excluded from the cruck province. Box-frame construction, unchallenged in the Eastern counties, is also found alongside cruck construction in the Midlands; even in the Northern and Western Counties, box-frame construction was often chosen in preference to cruck for buildings in the town and buildings for superior uses, such as the tithe barn of a great religious house. Hybrid forms of construction are found alongside the two pure techniques in the Midland Belt.

We have seen that the development of box-frame construction has continued almost to the present day. Cruck construction, once assumed to be exclusively a medieval technique, is now seen to have a continuous development, in raised crucks and upper crucks until well into the 19C.

54

a. diagram of cruck frame with two closed and one open truss

b. typical detail at corner showing cruck blade and wall post rising from a timber sill and stone plinth

c. rearing cruck trusses after assembly on the ground

d. roof covering in relation to cruck frame

e. diagram of box-frame two bays in length with posts and wall plates connected by tie beams and with a stud and rail infill wall

f. typical detail at corner showing post rising from a timber sill and supported by angle braces

g. diagram showing sequence of assembly

h. roof covering in relation to box-frame

55

Timber Walling

We have seen that, with reservations, a general structural distinction between cruck- and box-frame carpentry may be made. But timber external walls of cruck based, box-frame based, or hybrid construction, concealing the pure structural form of the building, appear to have characteristics of their own, according to recent research.

A distinction has been made between three schools of timber frame wall carpentry: a western school, characterized by squarish panels, short straight braces between post and wall plate, and the development of decorative timber around the panels; an eastern school, characterized by tall narrow panels and the use of curved braces between sill and post; and a less precisely defined northern school, characterized mainly by the omission of a sill between wall posts. The explanation of the difference in technique is, as yet, as obscure as the explanation for choice between cruck and other forms of timber construction.

Multi-storey construction in timber presented its own problems. When long straight timbers of substantial section were available, the constructional problems could be overcome, though at the cost of considerable waste of timber. But on restricted urban sites, and making use of shorter lengths of timber, jettied construction was adopted and spread as a fashion throughout most of the country. In jettied construction, floor beams were cantilevered to provide a base for the wall of each upper storey; with the use of dragon beams at the corners, jettied walls could be carried around adjacent sides of a building. The many-storied, multi-jettied half-timbered building represented the greatest flourish of heavy timber-framed wall construction but its origin and thorough explanation is still one of the greatest conundrums of the subject.

Western School
a. square panels
b. angle brace from
    post to wall
    plate
c. decorative members
    at corners
Eastern School
d. vertical panels
e. curved brace
    between post
    and sill
f. vertical panels
    with middle rail
Northern School
g. interrupted sill
(*a* to *g* after J. T.
    Smith)
See also distribution
    map
h. wall post and cruck
    blade (after
    F. W. B. Charles)
i. wall post and
    cruck blade
    (after Fox and
    Raglan)
j. jettied construction,
    eastern England
    (after T. L.
    Marsden)
k. dragon beam
    allowing heavy
    floor joists to
    project on two
    sides of a building
l. diagram showing
    sequence of
    erection of
    members of a
    jettied storey
m, n. details of jetties

57

Timber Walling: Wattle and Daub Infill

The material most commonly found as an infilling to the panels between the members of a timber frame wall was wattle and daub. In square panels, it was usual first to spring pointed staves between auger holes in an upper member and a slot in a lower to provide vertical bars, rather like the mullions of a window. These formed the warp between which a weft of pliable withies was woven in a basket weave pattern. On this wooden fabric a mixture of clay, dung, horsehair, etc., was daubed, and this was finished, inside and out, by a coat of plaster. As there might be decorative cusping or other patterns formed in the timber work, the shape of the panel would vary, but the technique was still followed.

Where, as in a barn, ventilation was more important than complete weather exclusion, then the daub and finish would be omitted. Where good quality timber was scarce the panels might be so large as to stretch like hurdles from post to post; then the daubing would be so thick as to make the technique more akin to a reinforced mud wall. It is possible, though evidence is as yet inadequate, that this form of infill preceded the division of timber walls into panels by means of studs and rails.

Other infill materials, such as thin stone slabs, tiles, and slate have been used, and when rendered are hard to distinguish from wattle and daub.

The contrasting black and white of pitch-coated timber and white-washed plaster gives the most spectacular results when this technique is used, but, except in the North Midlands, Cheshire, and Lancashire, a softer effect from naturally weathered oak and colour washed panels was more common.

a. The cutaway isometric shows, diagrammatically, the vertical studs and horizontal rails joined to make a square panel. Staves sprung into the underside of one rail and slotted into the top of another form a base for woven wattles. The daub on both sides is finished with a thin plaster coating.

b. Here the shape of the staves, and details at top and bottom are indicated.

c. An undaubed panel is illustrated, typical of the ventilator panels used in the wall of timber-framed barns in Hereford and Shropshire. There are many local variations of size and weave used in such panels.

d. For tall narrow panels laths may be sprung into grooves in studs and daubed.

e. Alternative for tall panels; laths woven around short staves sprung between auger holes and short grooves in the studs.

59

Timber Walling: Plain Tile Cladding

However pretty a half-timbered building might be, the thin panels of fragile wattle and daub were a poor weather protection, especially in exposed situations. When clay roofing tiles became cheap and easily available they were adopted as a cladding material over timber-framed walls.

The plain roofing tiles were hung on laths nailed to the wall timbers and other special tiles were moulded to cover the corners and jambs, or wooden cover moulds and architraves were used. Although the ordinary $10\frac{1}{2}$ in. by $6\frac{1}{2}$ in. roofing tile was most commonly used, other tiles with a shaped bottom edge were used to give decorative effects, and patterns were also derived from the use of differently coloured tiles. When tile cladding was added to existing buildings which had jettied upper floors, the opportunity was usually taken to build a new brick wall outside the lower framing timbers and in line with the tile hanging above.

Where tile hanging is carried down the face of a building this is usually an indication that the cladding was intended from the first. Indeed the material was an appropriate finish for the lightweight timber framing techniques which were being developed in South Eastern England during the early 19C. It has recently enjoyed a renaissance through use as a cladding for timber-framed industrialized housing and as an alternative cladding to give variety in school construction.

a. In the cutaway isometric, plain tiles are shown as a cladding to a heavy timber-framed wall. The tiles are hung on laths so so to give a triple lap, each tile covering two others. Where the members of the heavy frame were far apart intermediate studs are needed to help carry the laths. In light timber frame construction the closely spaced studs need no duplication.

b. and c. Here shaped and plain tiles are illustrated. Hand-made tiles usually had a camber in both directions; this helped to cover irregularities in the wooden wall.

d., e., f., g., h., i. Various shaped tiles are illustrated. They could be combined together, as in *g*, or with plain tiles, or in alternating colours to give an almost infinite series of variations.

Timber Walling: Mathematical Tile Cladding

Mathematical tiles (otherwise known as brick tiles or wall tiles) are like vertically hung roofing tiles but are shaped in section to imitate the header or stretcher face of a brick. They were nailed to timber boarding or hung on laths nailed to a timber-framed wall, like plain tiles, but had joints pointed in mortar like bricks. They gave a convincing imitation of a brick wall, especially when appropriately moulded tiles were used at corners and jambs.

Introduced towards the middle of the 18C., mathematical tiles were used in towns and villages throughout the South Eastern counties of England until well into the 19C. They provided a cheap means of giving a fashionable appearance to a timber-framed building though subject to the Brick Taxes. Usually the tiles were confined to the front elevation and, with plain tiles at the side and half timber at the rear of a building, the deception was not very serious. But when, in a town, only the front elevation was visible, the mathematical tiles were difficult to detect. At door and window openings, the usual details were replaced by imitations of stone dressings in painted wood or plaster or, not very convincingly, by scratching imitation voussoirs on the tiles. The natural red brick colour was usual, but greys, yellows, and even black, were also used.

Like plain tiles, mathematical tiles also served as the cladding for light timber-framed walls newly constructed in the early 19C., and they were used as a decorative covering to inferior materials such as flint or cobble.

a. In the cutaway isometric, mathematical tiles are shown as a cladding to a heavy timber-framed wall. The section shows how each tile was moulded to present a brick-like face, the body of the tile being fitted behind the other tiles which provided the lap. The tiles were hung or nailed to laths spanning between frame and studs. Alternatively (and perhaps more commonly) butt-edged boarding was nailed to the timber frame and the tiles were bedded in mortar and nailed to the boarding.

b. Specially shaped tiles were sometimes used at corners to help maintain the bond, and so preserve the illusion of brickwork.

c. Narrow tiles used as 'closers' in bonding were also used.

d. Timber cover strips were used to conceal joints between the tiles and other materials.

e. The detail around windows usually shows the shallow depth of a wall clad with mathematical tiles. Here the imitation brick arched head is really of painted plaster and the architraves are of wood.

f. Alternative sections of tiles.

Timber Walling: Weatherboard Cladding

The earliest adaptation of English building practices to American conditions made by the East Anglian settlers in New England was the use of clapboard or weatherboard as a cladding to their timber-framed buildings. The technique was not unknown in this country, and surviving examples suggest that weatherboards had been pegged to the framed walls of barns and other farm buildings at least from the late 16C., and to timber-framed church towers earlier still. But the technique never seems to have been popular for domestic buildings until weatherboarding was adopted as one of the cladding materials for lightweight timber-framed construction in South Eastern England towards the end of the 18C. Even then, use was practically confined to Cottages, and a few Small Houses, in domestic architecture, though the technique was popular for the timber-framed buildings for agriculture, transport and commerce.

Early weatherboarding was of oak or elm and was pegged to the timbers, but deal, nailed to studs, was used in the later phases. In this country, horizontal weatherboarding was customary, though vertical boarding with a cover strip was sometimes used and vertical boarding had been used for the church towers.

There are a few examples in this country of the use of planed and painted timber in imitation of ashlar masonry, a technique used on the front elevation of a house with weatherboarding elsewhere. It is a technique which was widely used in North America, and George Washington's house at Mount Vernon is a famous example.

64

a. Weatherboards are shown here as a cladding to a timber-framed wall of fairly heavy section. The boards are shown as 'feather edged' and with a single lap, each board covering one below. Usually it was not necessary to provide battens as the boards could span between posts or studs.

b. Butt-edged boarding.

c. Parallel-faced boards.

d. As *a*. but with beaded edges.

e. Lapped boards.

f. Vertical boards, nailed to rails and with cover strips to the vertical joints.

65

Timber Walling: Plaster and Pargetting as Cladding

An unbroken weather protective cladding has several potential advantages over the wattle and daub or tile claddings normally used with timber walled buildings. This became available with the widespread use of lime plaster on wooden lath. The lath and plaster could be plain, decorated only with a white or colour wash, or it could be moulded in one of the various forms known collectively as pargetting. Examples of decorative pargetting may be as early as the late 16C., though the technique was most popular in the second half of the 17C. and it fell out of favour after the middle of the 18C. At this time plain plaster cladding renewed its following and it continued to be associated with new and refurbished timber frame construction except in the North and the West Midlands, where 'magpie' or black and white work remained in favour.

Given adequate maintenance, properly applied lath and plaster will remain perfectly waterproof, but penetration of dampness from behind or through cracks will quickly lead to deterioration of the plaster and its key to the laths. Heavily moulded pargetting is vulnerable to the weather and soon loses its crisp outline; the simpler combed or incised panels are better preserved. Both techniques were more commonly used in the towns and larger villages than in hamlets or on isolated farm-houses. The period of greatest use of plain plaster cladding corresponds with the greatest popularity of smooth stucco renderings to rubble or brick walls, and, except for the general flatness which comes from the shallow window reveals of a timber-framed building it is difficult to distinguish the one form of construction from the other.

a. In the cutaway isometric the use of plaster on riven timber laths is illustrated. The laths were nailed, closely spaced, to the studs and any necessary intermediate members of a frame. Plaster, in two coats was then applied to the outside. There would be a separate lath and plaster interior lining. The illustration shows plaster cladding to an existing heavy timbered building, but the technique was also used with lightweight timber frame.

b. detail of plaster and laths.

c. basket weave combed pattern.

d. herring-bone combed pattern.

e. cable moulded and combed pattern.

f. fan combed pattern.

g. moulded pargetting, debased medieval pattern.

h. moulded panel pargetting

i. fleur-de-lis motif in pargetting.

Other Cladding Materials

Occasionally roofing slates were used as a cladding to timber-framed buildings. They were cut as small slates then nailed to laths and so to the timber frame, and they often included decorative patterns. The technique was found in towns and villages of the South West of England and is quite common across the Channel in Brittany. Slates were also used in North Wales and the Lake District as a weather-protective skin to stone walled buildings, especially to exposed gables.

A curious example, possibly unique, of a cladding to timber frame occurs in Kendal, Westmorland, where cast-iron plates appear to have been hung on to a timber frame. One of the plates carries the date 1853. The technique is related to the widespread practice in North America of the same period when cast-iron mouldings were used to give an imitation of Italianate masonry to timber-framed buildings.

Mud and Stud

A technique akin to conventional timber framing was used on humble buildings such as cottages and cowsheds at a fairly late date. A slender frame of rough timbers had walls made of staves thickly plastered with mud. Unlike half-timbering, the storey-height and bay-width panels were not divided by exposed studs and rails; unlike clay walling, the panels were only about 4 ins. thick and reinforced by the staves; but sometimes, like plaster cladding the covering was carried over the structural frame. Examples are known in Lincolnshire and coastal Lancashire but the technique may have been more widely used.

a. The isometric sketch shows the use of slates hung by nails on to laths spanning from post to post. The slates may have a single or double lap, according to the exposure of the situation.

b. Detail of a slate shaped at the bottom for use in decorative patterns.

c. Simple lozenge type pattern.

d. Composite pattern of slates.

e. Cast-iron panels applied to timber frame.

f. Framing for a two-bay mud and stud building.

g. Detail to show stave reinforcement for daubed mud.

69

Timber Walling With Brick Nogging

Many black and white timber houses prove on closer inspection to have the panels between their timbers infilled not with wattle and daub but with whitewashed brickwork. It is difficult at first view to decide whether this was an original filling or a later replacement. If closer examination shows that the auger holes and slots for staves were included in the timber then obviously the bricks have replaced wattle and daub, but brick nogging is in fact quite an old established practice. Apart from its possible use in medieval town houses, examples are beginning to come to light in the villages. In two timber-framed houses near Lutterworth, for example, one has the date 1695 scratched into one of the infill bricks, the other has the initials I B D and the date 1712 picked out in patterned bricks. In both examples the dates are consistent with the general character of the house and its construction.

Brick nogging is most appropriate to square panels, but other materials, such as tiles, slate, and thin stone slabs, have been used in tall narrow panels. Bricks were arranged in herring-bone fashion, diagonally and vertically as well as in the more customary fashion.

The understanding that brick panels could help to carry some of the loads in a wall must surely have helped to change the attitude among carpenters towards thinking of the wall acting as a whole, rather than as a separate series of posts. It certainly accompanied a reduction in the amount of timber used in the walls.

a. The isometric shows brickwork conventionally laid in courses as the infill to a heavy timber frame. Herring-bone brickwork was sometimes easier to fit into the panels as well as being more decorative. Brick-on-edge was used with lighter timber sections.

b. herring-bone brick infill.

c. stone or slate pieces in narrow panels between closely-spaced studs.

d. elevation of an early 18C. timber-framed Small House with brick nogging infill, including initials and date picked out in coloured bricks.

a

b   c

d

2. ROOFING: SHAPE, CONSTRUCTION AND MATERIALS

The intimate connection between roof and wall construction has already been discussed. Vernacular designers were constantly faced with the problem of choosing a sufficiently weatherproof covering and an appropriate form of roof construction to take it. Their choice was affected by the difficulty of relating suitable roof shapes to desired plan shapes and the increasing difficulty of achieving roof spans which were either greater than the length of available timber or which had to be constructed without obstructing the headroom in the rooms below. The record of their choice of roof covering is on external display. The history of roof construction is on view in open halls or repays exploration over plastered ceilings.

There are several basic distinctions which should be made, at the outset, before discussion of roof construction. In the first place a roof may be *single*, i.e. consisting only of rafters (with various bracing members) or it may be *double*, i.e. consisting of rafters and purlins. Secondly a roof may be divided into *bays* by *trusses*, or it may run uninterruptedly from end to end. (A double roof, for instance may consist of purlins spanning from wall to wall without intermediate support, or those purlins may be supported along their length by framed trusses of heavier timber. In such a case the purlin would normally be divided into separate lengths joined at the truss.) Thirdly a roof may be considered as a *rafter roof*, a *butt purlin roof*, or a *through purlin roof*. In a rafter single roof each pair of rafters is either without triangulation or is triangulated separately from every other pair of rafters; in a rafter double roof each pair of rafters is supported by purlins, either directly or indirectly, as when a purlin supports the collar of each individually triangulated set of rafters. A butt purlin roof consists of a series of trusses between which span purlins which are butted (or, more correctly, tenoned) into the principal rafters of the truss. A through purlin roof—and most crucks have through purlins—consists of a series of trusses supporting purlins which either rest simply on top of the blades of the truss, or are trenched into those blades. Fourthly, there are some roofs which incorporate parts of various of these categories.

The exact basis of roof construction, especially during the medieval period, has still not been satisfactorily revealed in spite of the best efforts of both architects and historians.

There is obvious relevance in the separate cruck- and box-frame traditions of timber frame construction, but recent research has tended to blur rather than clarify distinction between the two, while also suggesting that techniques of wall construction seem to be distinct from those of roof construction. However a fair understanding of what the carpenters thought they were doing may be gained by applying the observation that all members were thought to be acting in compression or were purely decorative, and that the medieval carpenters seemed to be preoccupied with the task of reducing unsupported spans.

The restrictions imposed by the various types of roof construction on plan shapes were only removed with the recent adoption of the flat roof. The simplest roof was that covering a rectangular plan, and the picturesque and irregular plans of some surviving buildings are the result of additions and subtraction rather than original intention. Roofs were, therefore, combinations of double pitch against double pitch. Roof construction also had some effect on sectional form. One obvious example is the use of the 'catslide' extension of the main roof over an outshut at side or end; another is the modification of roofs to light loft spaces. The choice of roof covering affected roof construction in that each material had its appropriate pitch, and the weight of a roofing material affected the required dimensions of roof timbers. The choice of roof covering also affected roof shape in that thatch and plain tiles, for instance, were easy to form into hips, whereas slate and pantiles were more appropriate to gabled roofs. Finally it is clear that, even at the vernacular level, fashion played its part, both locally in variations in decorative thatching (probably competitive) and nationally in the desire sometimes to hide a low-pitched slated roof behind a parapet in order to give the illusion of a flat roof.

Since the roof covering is especially vulnerable it will have been changed at least once in the lifetime of very many houses. Often the opportunity was taken to alter the roof construction or sectional form at the same time.

Roofing: shape, gable and eaves details

The actual shape of a roof varies basically according to membership of the hipped roof family or the gabled roof family. In the former the roof slopes in from all sides of the building; in the latter a pair of opposite walls continues up, above the eaves. There are several variations within the families; roofs begin as hips and end as gables and vice versa. Because of the special weather protection problems of a gable wall, various special details, e.g. 'tumbling-in' of brickwork have been developed.

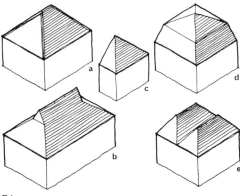

hipped roof family.
a. hipped roof.
b. gablet roof.
c. hipped roof on a projection.
d. hipped gambrel (mansard) roof.
e. hipped M-shaped roof.

Gabled roof family
a. gabled roof.
b. gabled roof on a projection.
c. gabled gambrel (mansard) roof.
d. half-hipped roof.
e. gabled single pitch roof.
f. gabled M-shaped roof.

Some Variations at the gable
g. 'Dutch' gable.
h. parapet at gable.
i. coping at gable.
j. plain close verge.
k. 'tumbling' in at gable.
l. 'kneeler' forming a termination at the eaves of a parapet or coping.
m. barge board.

Some Variations at the eaves
n. parapet at the eaves with rain-water head serving a concealed gutter.
o. exposed rafters at eaves.
p. cornice returned at gable.
q. plain close eaves.
r. wooden cornice serving as a gutter.

Roofing the double-pile plan
s. two gables at rear.
t. two hips at rear.
u. hips with flat centre section.
(M-shaped, gambrel and gabled roofs were also commonly used.)

Single and Double Rafter Roofs

Some of the common forms of single and double rafter roofs are illustrated. In this type of roof construction a ridge is uncommon; pairs of rafters were usually halved and pegged at the apex of the roof. Where the roof was carried on a thick wall, each rafter was usually triangulated at the foot by short members in the detail known as ashlaring. In rafter single roofs, the forest of rafters, collars, and braces often acted as studding for a ceiling of boards or plaster. In rafter double roofs such a ceiling is not often found, instead the exposed tie beam or arch braces may be decorated.

The most characteristic rafter double roof is the crown post roof in which a short post rises from the centre of a tie beam and carries a horizontal purlin or plate which in turn supports the collars of each individual set of rafters. The collar purlin was usually braced back to the crown post, and sometimes struts rise from the crown post to a collar.

a *collar rafter single roof* showing each pair of rafters separately triangulated and the absence of ridge and side purlins.

b. rafters halved and pegged together at the ridge.

c. dovetail halved joint between collar and rafter.

d. boarded ceiling giving the effect of a barrel vault.

e. ashlaring at junction of rafters.

f. junction between post, wall plate, and tie beam.

g. *crown post rafter double roof* showing crown post rising from tie beam to support a collar purlin which in turn supports collars and rafters.

h. crown post seen from below and showing the spread of the post to provide a seating for braces.

i. crown post seen from above to show the base swelling to meet a tie beam.

j. concave braces

k. convex braces

77

Aisled buildings

One way of increasing the useful floor area of a hall or barn was to add aisles on one or both sides and on one or both ends. Similarly, one way of spanning economically a given width of building was to introduce one or two sets of posts in order to reduce the unsupported span of roof beams. Some aisled cruck-framed buildings may be found, though aisles do not fit happily in the cruck tradition, but many aisled box-frame or post and truss buildings survive and evidence for the former existence of aisles may be seen in many more. Aisled halls appear to have been commonplace during the Middle Ages while aisled barns were still being erected well into the 18C. and possibly even into the 19C.

The essential feature of the aisled building is the arcade plate, a horizontal member running from post to post in the position of a wall plate but within the building. Arcade plates supported common rafters as they ran from the main roof to cover the aisles and were usually linked to the aisle posts both by the action of the joint at the end of each tie beam, and by the triangulation of straight or curved braces. In the earlier aisled buildings, transverse rigidity was given to the structure by means of passing braces: light timber members running along the surface of each main structural member.

Of necessity an arcade plate running from end to end of a building had to be assembled from several lengths of timber jointed end to end and carpenters used much ingenuity in devising various methods of joining or 'scarfing' the parts of the arcade plate—and other horizontal members.

Most aisled buildings are examples of 'normal assembly' in box-frame or post and truss construction, i.e. the head of the post carries both wall plate or arcade plate and tie beam, ingenious joints linking post, plate and beam as they run in three dimensions. Some aisled buildings, however, show 'reversed assembly', i.e. the wall plate is carried on the end of the tie beam which in turn is carried on the post.

a. isometric view of part of an aisled hall showing aisle post (1), arcade plate (2), wall plate (3), wall post (4) and cill (5), both the tie beam (6) and the arcade plate have braces running back to the aisle posts. The rafters which run from the ridge across the arcade plates to the wall plates, have been omitted in order to show the main structural members. *b.* cross section through an aisled hall showing a rafter roof with a collar purlin supported by a crown post rising from the tie beam. *c.* cross section to show the use of passing braces (1) running along the face of a series of members from wall post to rafter. *d.* scarf joint halved. *e.* scarf joint splayed and tabled. *f.* scarf joint lipped and halved. *g.* reversed assembly in which the wall plate is carried by the tie beam. *h.* normal assembly in which the tie beam is above the wall plate. *i.* flared jowl. *j.* jowl with taper and square-cut return. *k.* jowl with taper and curved return. *l.* no jowl at head of post.

Roof Construction: Butt Purlin Families

Where a roof includes rafters which are supported by purlins which in turn are supported by roof trusses, the form of the joint between purlin and truss is significant, and has been used as the key to the difference between two of the three main schools of roof carpentry. In the butt purlin roof, the purlins run between principal rafters in such a way that the top of the common rafters is in line with the top of the principal rafters; in other words the principal rafter acts also as a common rafter. In order to permit this combination, the purlin either passes right through the principal, or, more commonly, it is joined to the principal by a mortise and tenon joint. Sometimes the section of the principal is reduced at this point so that it continues to the ridge as a common rafter.

Butt purlin roofs are usually associated with box-frame timber construction, for the tie beam of the box-frame could act also as the tie beam of the roof truss. But often the tie beam was in an unsightly or inconvenient position, and various devices were adopted, both with timber and mass walls, to eliminate it. One popular device was to provide a collar at a higher level and use deep arch braces to help transfer roof loads well down the wall. Another was to eliminate the central portion of the tie beam, leaving the remainder as hammer beams, using short posts and arch braces to transmit loads from principal and collar respectively. A further, and rather confusing device, was to provide posts which curved inwards, like crucks, but which were topped by a collar or did not continue to a ridge; these base crucks seem to have been adopted sometimes to deal with erection problems. It was usual, though by no means universal, to halve the common rafters together rather than provide a ridge. Wind braces were sometimes provided, though whether the original purpose was lateral stability, decoration, or reduction of purlin span is not clear.

a. cutaway isometric showing butt-purlins (1) and a principal rafter reduced in section to terminate as a common rafter (2).

b. isometric showing butt-purlin, and sprocketed eaves.

c. butt-purlin passing through principal and scarfed between trusses.

d. butt-purlins tenoned into principal.

e. butt-purlin arch-braced collar truss.

f. butt-purlin hammer beams collar truss.

g. butt-purlin tie beam truss.

h. butt-purlin base cruck truss.

i. isometric showing the formation of the hammer beam (3) with the aid of the hammer post (4), wall piece (1), and an arch brace (2).

j. carrier butt purlin base cruck truss with inclined post in the form of a cruck blade (1), lower main collar (2), upper main collar (3), and subsidiary collar (4).

k. purlin clasped between collar and principal rafter.

l. purlin clasped as principal rafter is reduced to become a common rafter.

Roof Construction: Through Purlin Families

In contrast to the butt purlin roof, the purlins of a 'through purlin' roof are carried on the backs of the blades of the roof truss. The blade cannot act as a common rafter and indeed there is a space roughly corresponding to the depth of the purlin between the underside of the common rafter and the top of the blade. The side purlins may be carried on the top of a blade, kept in position by a block, or, more securely, they may be trenched into the top of the blade. In relatively crude construction, lengths of side purlin are lapped over each other at the blades, but, in superior work, scarfed joints link the lengths of purlin between trusses.

Though purlins are usually associated with cruck construction, the side purlins give intermediate support to common rafters which are also supported by a ridge purlin and wall plates. Because of the 'rearing' process involved in erecting a cruck truss, the joint at the head of the cruck blades was difficult to maintain, and several ways of dealing with the problem were devised. Again, because of the rearing process, the wall plate was most conveniently carried on top of the ends of a tie beam. Where, e.g. for reasons of headroom, the tie beam had been replaced by a collar at a higher level, then short cantilevered cruck spurs carried the wall plate. Where a wall of, e.g., stone or clay was considered capable of carrying the loads of a wall plate, the cruck spur might be entirely eliminated or a much more slender cruck tie used to maintain some link between wall plate and blade. Because the pitch of the roof was usually more shallow than the slope of the cruck blades, lower purlins were supported on separate blocking pieces or duplicate blades. So called 'wind braces' or 'sway braces' were often, though by no means invariably, provided to run diagonally between purlin and blade.

a. diagram showing the relationship between through purlins and cruck construction.

b. detail showing the relationship between through purlin, blade, and common rafters.

c. block carrying side purlin.

d. trenching for purlin.

e. closed cruck truss.

f. open cruck truss.

g. truncated cruck truss.

h. cruck spur.

i. cruck tie.

j. blades crossed at ridge.

k. blades halved at ridge.

l. plated yoke.

m. collar yoke.

n. link yoke.

o. saddle.

p. straight wind brace.

q. concave.

r. convex.

s. ogee.

t. reversed ogee.

u. double straight wind braces.

v. raised cruck truss.

w. upper cruck truss.

x. through purlin king post truss.

y. through purlin tie beam truss.

z. longitudinal support to ridge purlin.

aa. early king post (with stub tenon) resting on tie beam.

bb. late king post with strap tying post to tie beam.

83

Roofing Materials: Thatch

Thatch was formerly so universal a roofing material that the dialect word 'thack' is still applied to any roof covering. Although a great deal of thatch still remains—about 50,000 thatched buildings in England according to a recent estimate—replacement of thatch by Welsh slate, plain tile, and corrugated asbestos conceals the former use of the material over virtually the whole country.

The principal materials used were reed, straw, and heather, though other materials including turf and ling have been used at times. The best reed came from beds specially cultivated in Norfolk. Straw was usually wheaten, and combed wheat straw has similarities in use with reed, but rye straw was sometimes used. Heather was available in moorland areas where straw long enough for thatching was scarce. Threshing machines ruined straw for thatching purposes and there was presumably some relation between the spread of threshing machines in the north and west where other roofing materials were available, and their slow adoption in the east and south.

Thatch is a relatively light material, does not need a particularly massive roof construction, and can be used with poor walling materials such as mud or chalk. Often two courses of stone tiles were used at the wall head as a damp proof course over the most vulnerable part of the construction. The ridge was given extra protection by a further thickness of straw, often scalloped at the edge, and brought to a decorative peak at the apex. Hazel spars were used to give a great variety of decorative patterns at ridge, verge and eaves.

The nature of the material allowed valleys and dormers to be incorporated in the roof, and the soft, all-embracing lines of a thatched roof cannot be equalled in any other material.

a. The diagram shows various stages in thatching a roof with Norfolk reed. The basis having been formed with rafters and laths, a bunch is laid at the corner of the verge at 45°, other bunches are placed along the eaves, butt down, and, after tying, fixed with hazel sways. The brow course is neatly dressed into position.

b. A detail at the apex of a hipped roof in long straw.

c. A detail at the apex of a gabled roof in Norfolk reed with a scalloped edge and pattern of sways.

d. A thatched roof trapped between brick parapets.

e. A thatched roof over a cob building showing the easily swept shapes over a complex plan.

f. In a few humble cottages or farm buildings the thatch was carried not on rafters but on a pile of twigs or straw heaped on wattles and joists to make a roof shape (after D. M. Smith).

85

Roofing Materials: Slate

True slate is found in restricted areas of north and west Wales, Cornwall and Devon, Leicestershire, the Lake District, and the Isle of Man. The weight of the material and the difficulty of transport restricted its use to the vicinity of the quarries, or for exceptionally expensive buildings elsewhere. Improvements in water transport, both by coastal shipping and canals, during the second half of the 18C., led to increasing use, especially of the slate from the Lake District. The material was sought in towns as a substitute for inflammable thatch. However, rail transport during the second half of the 19C. led to the widespread use of Welsh Slate for all building types and in all districts.

Welsh Slate is usually used in thin slabs of uniform thickness and uniform size; courses are regular, and a roof slated with this material appears thin, smooth, and precise. The other slates are used in random widths and thicknesses, giving irregular courses, diminishing in depth from eaves to ridge. Both types are hung by nails on riven or sawn battens, and can be satisfactorily laid at pitches of 30° to 35°, though large Welsh Slates have been laid at an even lower pitch.

Slate is best used on gabled roofs with few valleys. Hips must either be covered by moulded hip tiles or hewn stone sections or they must be mitred in a flimsy and vulnerable fashion. Valleys require substantial and equally vulnerable lead gutters.

There seems little doubt that in the majority of roofs covered with Welsh Slates in English country districts—and in most Welsh country districts also—the material is a replacement for an earlier covering of thatch. The opportunity was often taken to raise the eaves and give greater height to upper floor bedrooms.

86

a. The cutaway diagram shows rafters, ridge piece, laths laid at an interval diminishing towards the ridge, and the slates, random in width and reducing in length to form diminishing courses. The ridge is covered by sections of stone cut to shape and bedded in mortar.

b. Lake District type slates, rough in section, random width, diminishing courses.

c. Welsh Slate, smooth in section, uniform width, even courses.

d. ridge of 'wrestler' slates.

e. stone ridge.

f. lead ridge.

g. tiled hip.

h. mitred slate hip with concealed lead soakers.

i. rough slate, head nailed.

j. smooth, precisely cut slate, centre nailed.

87

Roofing Materials: Stone Flags and Stone Tiles

Based to some extent on local terminology, a distinction is made here between stone flags—thick, heavy, roofing slabs found chiefly in the Pennines, and stone tiles—the thinner, lighter, stone roofing material of the Cotswolds and elsewhere in England and Wales. Most stone flags are basically sandstone in origin, and they include the products of the Kerridge quarries which roofed much of north-east Cheshire; most stone tiles are basically limestone in formation and include the well-known Clipsham tiles of Rutland.

The method of laying the roofing material was similar in both versions: each tile or flag was pegged by an oaken peg (or a sheep's bone peg in the Lake District) to a stout lath, pegged or nailed in turn to the rafters; diminishing courses were used, and the top of each tile was usually rounded off, presumably to help reduce weight. The underside of the roof covering was often 'torched' with a mixture of clay and hair in order to reduce draughts and the penetration of snow.

Stone flags were usually laid to a low pitch of about 30°. They were graduated in size from slabs as much as four feet wide and three inches thick at the eaves to quite tiny, thin slabs at the ridge. They were used only on simple broad surfaces of roof. Stone tiles, however, were usually laid to a much steeper pitch, 50° or even more, their graduation was less marked, and the smaller tiles, swept around valleys, gave intricate roof shapes of quite a delicate effect.

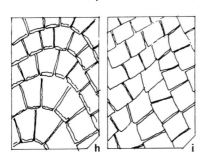

a. The diagram shows a roof of rafters, ridge purlin, and laths laid in diminishing courses with stone flags held in position by wooden pegs (or sheep's bones)
b. stone tile with lap over.
c. stone flag with lap over.
d. stone tile showing rough texture.
e. stone flag showing smooth but bold texture.
f. stone flags laid, at the eaves, beneath a thatched roof.
g. stone flags laid at the eaves of a tiled or slated roof.
h. stone tiles swept round a valley.
i. stone tiles laced up a valley.

Roofing Materials: Plain Tiles

The manufacture and use of clay plain tiles has marched along with the development of brick making. The size of the plain tile, $10\frac{1}{2}$ in. by $6\frac{1}{2}$ in. by $\frac{1}{2}$ in. was standardized in 1477 and its use, like that of brick for walling, was at first confined to the Eastern and South-Eastern Counties. Like brick, tiles were favoured in the towns as a fire-resistant material, and their use spread wherever slate or stone was not available.

Plain tiles were nailed, or were hung by means of nibs, moulded into the tile, from light battens. They were laid in regular courses but, in order to protect the joints between tiles, each tile lapped two others, leaving only about four inches exposed and the tiles were usually laid at a pitch of more than 45°. By means of specially moulded hip and valley tiles it was quite satisfactory to cover intricate roof shapes with plain tiles.

Early plain tiles were hand-made and the exaggerated camber in both the length and breadth of the tile gave an intricate character to an old tiled roof which a modern roof in the same material entirely lacks. Later developments included the use of multi-coloured tiles in order to display pattern, dates, and initials in the roof, as well as the use of specially shaped tiles to give varying textures and patterns.

a. the cutaway diagram shows rafters halved at the ridge, laths laid at a regular interval from eaves to ridge, and plain tiles, each one overlapping two others so that there is a thickness of three tiles at each joint. The ridge is a half-round tile.

b. decorative tiling in alternate colours.

c. decorative tiling in alternate courses of different colours.

d. alternate courses of plain and shaped tiles.

e. fishscale tiles.

f. size of tile.

g. tile and a half for closing at eaves.

h. underside of tile showing nibs and nail holes.

i. hips formed of shaped hip tiles.

j. hips formed of bonnet hip tiles.

Roofing Materials: Pantiles

The Pantile resembles the plain tile in material and manufacture but differs in form and use. The size of a pantile, 13½ in. by 9½ in. by ½ in., was fixed during the reign of George I, pantiles having been imported from Holland, certainly towards the end of the 17C., probably before, and local manufacture having started at the beginning of the 18C. They quickly spread over the whole of the Eastern Counties north of London right up to the Scottish border. Except for a strong tradition in Bridgwater, Somerset, pantiles are virtually unknown in the western half of the country.

Pantiles are single lap tiles in the sense that each tile laps over only one tile beneath, but the side joints, so vulnerable in plain tiles, are protected by a sideways lap, permitted by the flat S section of the tile. They could be laid to a low pitch of 30°–35°, provided a lightweight roof and required a relatively insubstantial roof structure. The underside of the pantiles was usually torched with clay to reduce snow penetration.

The bold form of a pantiled roof is best used in simple shapes as hips and valleys and small roof sections generally are difficult to form; the verge of a pantiled roof is often protected by a low parapet.

Other forms of single lap tile, such as Roman and Spanish tiles, have not formed any significant part of the British vernacular tradition.

a. The cutaway diagram shows rafters halved at the ridge, widely spaced laths, and pantiles lapping sideways and at each course, together with half-round ridge tile.
b. detail of the pantile and the sideways lap.
c. detail showing gable carried up as a parapet and half-round ridge tiles with galletting of small pieces of plain tile.
d. hip with half-round ridge tiles.
e. detail of torching.

Roofing: Chimneys

Just as the relationship between fireplace and entrance is one of the two major factors governing plan arrangement in vernacular houses, so is the relationship between chimney and roof a major determinant in the external appearance of such a building.

A chimney can be located so as to pass through the ridge, at a gable, at the eaves on side or end of a hipped roof, or through some point part way along the slope of a roof. Each location has a meaning on plan and created problems in construction.

A chimney passing through the ridge meant that little of the chimney stack need be exposed to the weather, and weather proofing problems were minimized; earlier chimneys projected from the gable wall and were kept clear of inflammable thatch; at the eaves chimneys were clear of thatch, but the joint with the roof material collected rainwater unless protected by a tiny roof pitched opposite to the main roof; part way up the pitch meant waterproofing problems and yet was often unavoidable because of planning requirements.

Chimney stacks were made of brick or stone according to the material available locally. Brick was the most satisfactory material, and gave the opportunity for splendid displays of craftsmanship. Dressed stone suffered from the heat and water penetration but provided good opportunities for decoration; undressed stone was difficult to use for chimney stacks, and the circular stacks of Pembroke and parts of the Lake District were an attempt to avoid the jointing problems at corners.

Although chimney pots have been used for superior houses from the early medieval period they were rarely used at the vernacular level. Most chimney pots now seen are 19C. work and it is doubtful if devices like the inclined slates of the Lake District are much older.

94

a. positions for chimneys
1. projecting from gable.
2. projecting at first floor from gable.
3. projecting from side wall.
4. in gable wall.
5. within the house, passing through the ridge.
6. within the house, avoiding the ridge.

b. stone chimney stacks
1. panelled stack, on a base.
2. circular stack of small stones.
3. square stack with water tabling to protect the joint between stack and roof.

c. brick chimney stacks
1. two flues with decorative shape on plan and use of oversailing brick courses.
2. separate stack projecting from side wall, tumbled-in brickwork, small gabled roof masking joint with main roof.

d. various chimney pots.
1. slate or stone on short pillars; found in Devon.
2. common tapered tile pot.
3. inclined slates as in the Lake District.
4. medieval tile pot.

95

Roofing: Dormers

Dormer windows may be contained entirely in the roof slope or may include some vertical continuation of the house wall. In either variety they serve to provide light to rooms contained partly in the roof space.

The gradual development of the loft into a full height first floor will later be noted. Light could be provided to the end rooms by means of windows in the gables; for the centre rooms and in hipped roofs light was obtained from dormer windows. Where loft space was the result of inserting a floor into a room originally open to the roof, dormers would be inserted at the same time. Where architectural fashion required the roof slope to be hidden behind a parapet, or a strong horizontal cornice to be included at eaves level in order to complete the architectural composition of an elevation, then, again, dormer windows would serve the top floor.

Generally, in vernacular work, the main roofing material was continued over dormers. In thatched roofs this was conveniently and agreeably done by sweeping the thatch over 'eyebrow' windows or around full dormers; in stone tiled roofs, swept or laced valleys continued the coursing of tiles neatly over dormers. In plain tiled roofs, specially shaped valley tiles linked major and minor roofs, but pantiles, slates, and stone flags required lead valleys to separate the roof of the dormer from the main roof. At the same time the roof of the dormer tends to follow that of the main roof, hips with hips and gables with gables.

One alternative way of providing light to a loft was by means of a roof light, following the slope of the main roof, and this was often associated with top floor workshops in the early 19C.

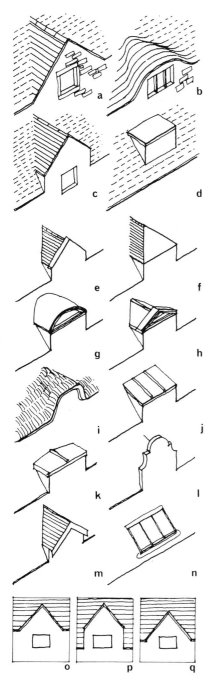

a. gabled dormer, window above eaves.
b. eyebrow dormer at eaves.
c. gabled dormer window partly below eaves.
d. dormer wholly in roof space.
e. gabled dormer with plain coping.
f. hipped dormer.
g. segmental pediment to dormer.
h. triangular pediment to dormer.
i. thatched hood to dormer.
j. sloping lead roof to dormer.
k. flat lead roof to dormer.
l. 'Dutch' gable to dormer.
m. bargeboards to dormer gable.
n. sloping rooflight.
o., p., q. distinguish between dormer windows below, above, and across the eaves line.

3. PLAN AND SECTION

In this chapter the different forms of plan and section commonly found in vernacular houses are examined, together with the forms of staircase which usually relate plan to section. The three items are considered together as, even in such simple buildings, they are inextricably linked, any designer of a multi-storey structure having to think simultaneously of plan, section, and staircases, and to acknowledge that modification of one element has its repercussions on the other two.

Consideration of plan form occupies the major part of this chapter as it so often represents the culminating phase in any study of vernacular architecture. Those students who are especially concerned with the way of life enshrined in an example of minor domestic architecture will be primarily interested in plans and will consider architectural details, building materials, and forms of construction, as ways of establishing and explaining the plan form at various periods. Recently, attempts have been made to set up a classification of vernacular plan forms, and we are approaching the time when such a classification, capable of national application, can be accepted. Against this, individual examples may be set and regional and local variations established. It is possible that in so doing we will find rather less local variation in plan form than was once expected.

The elements of plan and sectional form at the vernacular level are very few. Whatever the local variations, the permutations of these few elements adopted nationally from time to time are surprisingly numerous.

While some examples of a single build may illustrate the plan and sectional form appropriate to a particular family in a particular place and at a particular time, many examples show the development from one plan or cross-section to another. By examining changes in material and structure one may determine how simple or archaic plans were extended at side and rear to form new plans while single-storey buildings were extended upwards to provide extra levels of accommodation. In addition, of course, houses were 'modernized' through alterations to window shape or door position without alterations to plan and section, and this process still continues.

Plan Forms: Introduction

It has already been suggested that plan and sectional form are inextricably linked and yet some attempt should be made to distinguish at least the ground floor plans to be commonly found.

The variations in plan form in domestic vernacular depend on the inter-relationship between the positions of the main hearth or fireplace, the main staircase, the main entrance, and the overall plan shape. Some of these components can be fairly reliably detected from outside the house: the front door and the general plan shape can be distinguished, the main chimney (which is not always the biggest) will usually still be in use, and a small 'fire window' may be present to confirm the position of the principal fireplace. The position of the staircase is usually less obvious unless it is contained in a projection or lit by a window at a half landing. Often, however, a house will show two or more phases of construction and these can usually be distinguished through changes of material on the exterior.

Apart from the plans which relate to first floor living, seven plan form families are here proposed. These families each contain many members, though there are also a few orphans to add to the numbers of individual plan variations. The classification, such as it is, will seem coarse when set against some of the other published classifications related to different regions of the country, but it is presented as a simple basis on which more detailed classifications may be established for each different locality.

Generally, projections or outshuts from the main plan shape have been ignored, but sometimes they are shown as essential to the organization of the plan.

Conventionally the 'upper' end of a house includes the more private rooms—parlours, etc.—while the 'lower' end is closest to the cooking, cleaning, and dirty operations of the household, and closest to the farm buildings; in fact, where a house is built across a slope, the upper and lower in status usually correspond to the slope of the ground.

For each plan form a diagram has been prepared to show position of fireplace, door, and staircase in relation to the ground floor plan shape; other elements such as windows and subsidiary doors have been ignored. Smaller, even more diagrammatic, plans have been added to show the common variations. Generally the first floor plan has been ignored.

Although most of the diagrams are based on stone walled buildings, the plans were equally appropriate to other materials.

Plan Form Families:
The First Floor Family

First floor living may be either patrician or defensive in origin. Two versions appear at the vernacular level: the tower house and the upper floor hall house.

In the basic *tower house*, the main living-room occupies the first floor, private rooms and bedrooms occupy the second and any higher floors, while the ground floor contains service or storage space. Usually the living-room was heated by a mural fireplace. Connection between the floors was by a spiral staircase in one corner of the tower, entrance was normally at first floor level, though it could be from the ground floor, and staircases were alternatively placed in a projecting turret or were fitted as straight flights into the thickness of the wall.

In the basic *upper floor hall house*, the first floor was occupied by a larger, general living-room, and a smaller private room. Above were subsidiary bedrooms in a full storey or garret space. It is generally assumed that the ground floor was used for storage, though in the bastel house version it is believed to have accommodated cattle. It is, however, possible that the ground floor was used for subsidiary living accommodation. The principal fireplace was located in the first floor hall, either on a side or an end wall, and sometimes there was a small fireplace in the private room. Entrance was normally by means of an outside staircase on the front wall.

Tower houses were common on the Scottish border but several examples have recently come to light on both sides of the Welsh border. Upper floor hall houses remain in small numbers from Norman times, but most of the surviving examples in Northumberland and Cumberland and, again, in parts of Wales, appear to date from the mid-14C. and mid-16C.

a. tower house, vaulted ground floor, typical upper floor, and battlemented roof. *b.* corner staircase. *c.* mural straight flight staircase. *d.* staircase in projecting turret. *e.,f.* alternative fireplace positions. *g.* alternative ground floor. *h.* upper floor hall house (bastel house if defensible), ground floor and first floor. *i., j.* alternative fireplace positions. *k.* alternative staircase position.

Plan Form Families: The Hall Family

The Hall family comprises all those house plans in which the principal ground floor living-room is open to the roof, together with such plans as retain a room similar in position and function but ceiled. There are two main versions: the single-ended and the double-ended halls.

In the *single-ended hall* plan a two-storey wing is attached to one end of an open hall. This wing usually projects beyond the side wall of the hall but may only project in one direction or even have no projection at all apart, possibly, from a jettied upper storey. There is usually a cross passage between hall and wing, but this may be found to have been blocked by the insertion of a later fireplace. Alternative fireplace positions include the long wall, against the cross passage, or at the exposed end of the hall. The staircase is usually contained entirely in the wing.

In the *double-ended hall* plan, an open hall is flanked by two multi-storey wings. These may be marked externally by no more than jettied upper floors as in the so-called Wealden plan, may have a bold gabled projection, as in the clothiers' houses of the West Riding, or may be extended to give a U-shape, as in some late examples in Cambridgeshire. There is usually a cross-passage, the 'screens passage', at one end of the hall, off which open buttery and pantry and a passage leading to an out-side kitchen. At the other end a staircase gives access to a first floor private chamber. Early examples have an open hearth in the hall but this has usually been replaced by a side or end wall fireplace.

Both single-ended and double-ended halls may be found in all parts of the country and the plan form, originating at the highest levels of society, passed eventually to the lower ranges of the social scale.

a. a house with open hall; the version illustrated has two rooms and a cross passage at the lower end, an open hall, and one room at the upper end; the cruck trusses include an open truss over the hall. *b.* example of a small hall house with open hearth near the cross passage. *c.* aisled hall. *d.* single-ended hall, the open hall and cross passage is shown attached to a wing with buttery, pantry, and kitchen passage on the ground floor and a solar above. *e., f., g.,* are alternative fireplace positions. *h., i.* are alternative staircase positions. *j.* a double ended hall, the open hall and cross passage are flanked at the lower end by a wing with buttery, pantry, and kitchen passage and a room above, and, at the upper end, by a store or private room with a solar above. *k., l.* are alternative fireplace positions. *m., n.* are alternative staircase positions. *o.* Wealden house.

Plan Form Families: The Two-Unit Family

This family comprises two groups of house plan—those consisting essentially of one structural cell divided by a partition into a larger and a smaller room and those in which a further unit is added at one end though with the interruption of a cross passage.

In the first group the larger room performed the function of the hall but was never open to the roof, having a bedroom or loft above; the smaller room acted as a private space and was itself often partitioned to give a small pantry separately entered from the living-room. Usually only the larger room was heated and this by a fireplace in an end wall. Sometimes the smaller room had a fireplace, though this was more likely to be a later addition than an original feature. The main entrance might be in the end wall, alongside the fireplace, at the fireplace end of the front wall, or about the centre of the front wall, near the partition (though in this last version of the plan there would not usually be a contemporary cross passage). The staircase was usually tucked into a recess alongside the fireplace on the end wall, although it might be set in a turret projecting from about the centre of the rear wall or even be taken out of a corner of the private end.

In the second group, the plan forms are similar except that an extension incorporating a cross passage was added to the lower end. Many examples of the first group have undoubtedly been extended to form the second, but it must be acknowledged that many more seem to have been so built from the beginning. The extra room was a service room (sometimes agricultural rather than domestic) and it might have a fireplace in the exposed gable wall. Sometimes the private room at the upper end of the basic plan was replaced by a wing at the rear.

104

a. the basic two-unit plan, with living-room, pantry, and parlour on the ground floor and bedrooms or a loft above. *b.* the two-unit plan with cross passage and service room added at the lower end. *c.* a modification of *b* with a cross passage and farm buildings added at the lower end, 'longhouse' style. *d.*, *e.* and *h.* are alternative fireplace positions, *i.* has two fireplaces. *l.*, *m.* are alternative staircase positions. *f.* and *g.* are alternative staircase positions to plan *b*. *j.* shows an additional fireplace at the upper end. *k.*, *n.* show additional fireplaces at the lower end. *o.* shows a parlour and fireplace projecting from the rear.

Plan Form Families: Central Fireplaces Family

In the *cenral fireplace* family the basic plan consists of an upper room, a living-room and a service room, with living and service rooms heated by two fireplaces back to back, and with the main entrance at the junction of these rooms where fireplace jambs and outer wall form a little lobby. Although having some superficial similarities to the two-unit plan family there is the important distinction that the fireplaces are set back to back and there is no cross passage. Variations from the basic plan depend, again, on the position of the staircase and other fireplaces. In some versions the upper room may be eliminated, its functions performed by upper floor rooms; in others the two main fireplaces heat living and private rooms while the service room projects from the rear. This family appears to be confined to Lowland England, especially the Eastern Counties, but was popular among 17C. New England colonists.

The most compact version, having only two rooms on the ground floor, could also be the most cramped and some examples were made more convenient and imposing through the use of a multi-storey porch at the front and a staircase projection at the rear.

While most examples of the central fireplace family have the two fireplaces built at one time, in some instances only one was provided initially and the other added later. This sequence may show on the outside of the building when the front door lies to one side of a line running from chimney stack to ground instead of in the middle of it.

The family is sometimes called *lobby entry* or *baffle entry*.

a. the basic plan with only two rooms on the ground floor: hall (1) and parlour (2) with lobby entrance (3) and, in this instance, a porch (4) and staircase projection (5). b. the basic plan with central fireplaces back-to-back, one serving the living-room which has unheated pantry and parlour opening off it, the other serving a service room. c. variation with living and service rooms and a central staircase. d,e,g,h. alternative staircase positions. f. additional service rooms in an outshut at the rear. i. single unit. j. single unit extended. k. back-to-back fireplaces without lobby entrance. l. staircase between fireplaces (flues join over).

Plan Form Families:
Inside Cross Passage Family

There is a plan form family which is characterized by a *passage* which runs *across the structural cell*. Partitioned off the passage, there are on one side unheated storage rooms (e.g. buttery and pantry) and, on the other side a passage which runs across the end of the principal living-room and opposite the main fireplace; private rooms and bedrooms are confined to the upper floors. Although the main fireplace is usually in the end wall of the living-room, it may be in the side wall in which case there may be a parlour at one end of the house. The staircase is usually to be found alongside the main fireplace but it may, in late examples, back on to the cross-passage. The plan form is not as common as some others, though many examples are to be seen in North Wales.

While the standard arrangement has a fireplace only at one end of the ground floor the principal chamber on the first floor at the opposite end is often provided with a fireplace. This projects slightly from the wall, the chimney breast being corbelled out at first floor level.

Plan Form Families: Central Service Room

Generally, unheated service rooms are placed at one end of the house: below a cross-passage, alongside a small parlour for instance, but there are some houses in which this room is placed in the middle of the house, between the two principal heated living rooms. It is rather as if a two-unit house had been stretched by the insertion of such a room. Where the entrance was at the centre of the main elevation, a compact lobby gave access to the two rooms and the service room, an arrangement which may well have appeared odd at a time when one room usually opened off another.

Examples of this plan are not especially numerous or widespread but they may be seen in the southern half of Wales and in the South-West of England.

a. the basic inside cross-passage plan ground floor. *b.* first floor of the basic plan showing projecting chimney breast. *c.* isometric sketch of an example of this plan. *d.* alternative fireplace position. *e.* alternative with two gable ground floor fireplaces. *f.* two fireplaces and the passage across the main room. *g.* two fireplaces and the passage in the normal position. *h.* the basic central service room plan. *i.* alternative with gable entry.

Plan Form Families: Side Wall Fireplace Plans

When the open hearth fell out of favour and was replaced by a fireplace, there were two positions in which that fireplace could be located: on an end wall facing along the length of the hall, or on a side wall facing across the hall. In the majority of smaller houses the former position was chosen; in the majority of larger houses the choice fell on the latter position. In the small houses the fireplace could be conveniently located to back onto a cross-passage (if this were to be retained) or could be so located in a redundant cross-passage as to give the greatest possible useful floor space to the hall. In the larger houses, with correspondingly larger rooms, the best distribution of heat came from a position at the middle of a side wall. Usually the rear side wall was chosen for the fireplace and this gave the best impression to the visitor entering through the front door and between the screens. In a number of small houses, concentrated mainly in certain areas on each side of the Bristol Channel, the side wall was chosen but at the front of the house where, no doubt, the best possible impression was given to the visitor as the chimney breast and stack were the most prominent objects on the front elevation.

The plan whose distinguishing feature was the fireplace on the front side wall, alongside the entrance doorway, is associated with the longhouse arrangement occasionally, with other two-unit plans, but mainly with houses of three units. Welsh examples may either have the service room beyond the cross-passage or a heated parlour, and the latter arrangement has been found to be the most common. In Wales, especially, the front chimney is given even greater emphasis by the tall chimney stack.

Houses of this type appear to date from the late 16C. and the plan was used throughout the 17C. and into the 18C. These are the dates of transformation of older houses as well as new construction on the same plan. There is a heavy concentration in Pembrokeshire, but the plan is also used in other parts of the Welsh side of the Bristol Channel; there are also numerous examples in North Devon stretching both into Somerset and Cornwall, and also down into South Devon near Exeter.

a. front fireplace serving hall which incorporates cross-passage; parlour beyond the passage. *b.* front fireplace serving hall, true cross-passage, parlour beyond hall, service room beyond passage. *c.* sketch to show front side wall fireplace, chimney breast and stack. *d.* front side wall fireplace as part of longhouse (animals beyond cross-passage) (cf. Alcock, Sanders, Lettaford). *e.* two units with inside cross-passage and front fireplace (cf. Williams, Poltimore, Farway).

Plan Form Families: The Double Pile Plans

The essential characteristic of the double pile plan is that it is entirely two rooms in depth. In all other plans the principal room has run through from front to back walls, even though subsidiary rooms may only have occupied part of the depth of the building.

The basic version of the double pile plan consists of four rooms, a principal living-room, a private room, a kitchen, and another service room (e.g. a dairy or a pantry). A staircase at the rear between the two subsidiary rooms rises to the upper floors. Fireplaces, which are usually provided to all rooms except the service room, are built into the end walls. The front door is placed close to the centre of the main elevation, and a lobby serving the entrance, the staircase and all four rooms was, in the larger and later examples, partitioned off the main living-room. As an alternative, especially in Eastern England, the fireplaces may be found placed back-to-back on partition walls. In another example the staircase rises between the two principal rooms. Where further accommodation was needed, then a sideways extension was provided, with its own fireplaces and even, sometimes, its own staircase.

While the basic version of the double pile plan gave the effect known to house agents as 'double-fronted', half the plan gave the 'single-fronted' elevation commonly found in urban terraces and rural cottages. In this variation there are two rooms on each floor, not four, and extensions could be made at the rear, as in the 'tunnel back' town houses.

The double pile plan was introduced high in the social scale towards the beginning of the 17C., by the middle of the 18C. it had spread to all parts of the country and all levels of society.

a. first floor and *b*. ground floor, double-fronted.   *c*. ground floor, single-fronted.   *d*. and *e*. alternative fireplace and staircase positions.   *f*. and *g*. alternative staircase positions, single-fronted.   *h*. double-fronted extended by an additional unit.   *i*. back-to-back single-fronted.   *j*. extension at the rear of a single-fronted cottage, the 'tunnel back'.   *k, l, m*. plan, front and rear view of continuous outshut predecessor to double pile plans.

Sectional Form: Introduction

Some of the earliest surviving examples of minor domestic architecture were designed for first floor living. These might be tower houses, with the main living-room on the first floor, private rooms above, and service rooms below—for such houses continued to be built at the vernacular level until the early 17C.—or they might be houses with a living-room and private rooms on the first floor and service rooms beneath, having a long history stretching from Norman times until Elizabethan. But with these exceptions the story of vernacular architecture is one of modification and adaptation based on ground floor living.

The open hall, a ground floor room open to the roof timbers, seems to be the vernacular counterpart of the Saxon communal hall. The evidence from excavations as well as examination of surviving fragments suggests that the aisled open hall was once in common use, at least in the eastern half of the country, to accommodate all living quarters, but the earliest surviving examples of the open hall, aisled or not, are combined with a two-storey wing. In such a wing the room on the upper floor was normally the most important and might itself be open to a roof of decorated timbers. The open hall remained in use at a steadily decreasing social level until the 19C., when the principal living-room of a quarryman's cottage might be open to its roof.

However fine the architectural qualities of an open hall, the physical discomforts were considerable and, percolating gradually down the social scale, it became customary to insert an intermediate floor over the whole house. At the inferior social levels the principal bedroom remained on the ground floor and the upper storey was an ill-lit loft, cramped and with inadequate headroom. However, by using dormer windows or by raising the eaves and altering the roof construction, a more commodious upper floor was made possible and eventually became the bedroom floor.

Even the two-storey house usually had a garret space available for storage, for servants' accommodation, or for other service functions.

Open Hall

a. The open hall was originally associated with the open hearth which, in superior buildings would be in the centre of the room but which was more likely to be to one side in vernacular buildings. Smoke would be allowed to escape through special ridge tiles, timbered louvres at the ridge, louvred gablets, or unglazed windows; a coved canopy protected the upper end of the hall against soot and downdraughts.

b. The most common type of open hall had a cross-passage at the lower end with doors to buttery, pantry and kitchen. The hall was screened by a partition or 'spere' with two doors leading in to the cross-passage. In the North and West there was often a spere truss with fixed partitions at each end and a moveable screen between.

c. Even after the central hearth had been abandoned the open hall remained in use with the fire either contained in a conventional fireplace with flue and chimney or set against a wall and with smoke collected in a hood usually of studs and thick daub though sometimes of stone. In some districts platforms on each side of the hood provided storage space or even beds.

d. The 'croglofft' cottage had a single room open to a low roof. At the 'upper' end, opposite the hearth, a cubicle was partitioned off, partly with furniture, above this was a low loft reached by a ladder. This is probably a late and rude survival of the process by which the hall was eventually floored.

One and a half storey

a. The two obstacles to full use of the loft space over a rectangular house were difficulties in lighting and lack of headroom. In a house with a gabled or half-hipped roof, light could be fairly easily obtained from the end walls. Light from side walls could only be obtained with the use of dormer windows or by raising eaves to allow for low-level window.

b. In the example illustrated the ground floor has full height but the loft space above is low and cramped. The collar rafter roof eliminates obstructive beams and the gable window provides some light but the eaves are too low to enable the centre of the loft to be daylit.

c. Here, one of the many types of dormer window is illustrated in half the section. In this type the main wall has been carried up to provide the window and the dormer has been roofed in a flatter continuation of the main roof. The many other varieties of dormer are illustrated in another chapter. The other half of the section shows side windows down at floor level.

d. The upper cruck truss was one of the devices adopted to improve headroom. Others included the use of purlins carried on cross walls avoiding the need for trusses, and use of the double pitch or gambrel roof. Improved lighting and adequate headroom made possible the full use of an upper floor.

Multi-storey

a. The use of two full storeys allowed the principal bedroom to move from the ground to the first floor. Consequently the two floors became comparable in importance and therefore similar in height. The prevailing fashion for lofty rooms and tall windows emphasized the change.

b. In many parts of the country, the adoption of a full-height first floor was accompanied by an extension of the ground floor by means of an 'outshut' at the rear. Some parts of such an outshut would be open to the roof, others would be ceiled to give small cramped storage places or bedroom lofts. These gradually passed through the same process of improving lighting and headroom as the main part of the house but quite often the rear part was rather lower than the front even when both had adequate height.

c. Use of the upper floors for storage and service functions continued after two full floors were in domestic use. The garret space was usually lit by small gable or dormer windows. Once cross-walls instead of trusses were used to carry purlins, the problems of headroom were reduced. In the example illustrated, such purlins permitted the unbroken floor space required by some types of cottage industry. Here light was obtained by a dormer window and by a rooflight of glass in a timber frame and following the roof slope.

d. Cellars were not often used in vernacular buildings unless the slope of the land or the pattern book examples called for them. Even in quite small and remote villages the influence of such books led to the occasional use of the 'piano nobile' and the more common use of an attic storey hidden behind a parapet.

Hearths, Smoke Bays and Fireplaces

Recent investigations, especially in Surrey, have shown that there were three distinct stages in the development of heating for Small Houses: use of the open hall, provision of a smoke bay or hood, and insertion of a fireplace.

In Wealden Houses, where a hall open to the roof was flanked by two-storey bays, smoke from an open fire collected in the roof space before emerging through a louvre, through gablets, or through the chinks in a tiled roof. As the partitions between hall and flanking bays were usually carried up to the ridge, smoke-blackening was present but confined to rafters over the hall. In some such houses, the chamber on the first floor of the socially superior end of the house was jettied into the hall rather than out to the front or the side. This idea was developed by introducing a chamber over the main part of the hall. A portion was left, however, to channel smoke into the roof and this 'smoke bay' confined blackening to certain rafters over the hearth and, usually, over the cross-passage. In some instances the smoke bay was also confined on one or both sides. Later the use of a brick fireplace, chimney breast, flue and chimney stack gave relatively efficient combustion, concentrated the fire and its attendant implements in one place, and allowed the chamber to be heated by an extra flue in the same stack. In existing houses it proved convenient to insert the fireplace in the cross-passage, using space no longer needed for control of draught to an open hearth. In new construction of the same period two fireplaces back to back serving the two principal ground floor rooms produced the central fireplaces (lobby entrance) plan.

118

a. cross-section through an open hall showing that smoke could ascend freely from the hearth to the roof. *b.* longitudinal section with smoke blackening on rafters above the hall (1). *c.* plan showing the hearth and the opposed doors which gave the effect of a cross-passage. (In this and other plans the position of the staircase is not indicated.) *d.* cross-section showing the smoke bay rising beyond the partition wall of the chamber over the hall. *e.* longitudinal section with smoke confined within the smoke bay (2). *f.* plan showing the smoke bay accommodating hearth and passage. *g.* cross-section to show an intermediate floor over the whole of the hall and the provision of ground and first floor fireplaces. The sketch indicates a chamber open to the roof but ceilings were usually introduced to improve the comfort of the room. *h.* longitudinal section showing fireplaces and flues. *i.* plan illustrating a large brick fireplace in the cross-passage; only one door is retained; the space between the fireplace and the rear wall was available for a staircase.

In the south and east there was usually nothing more than a timber framed partition between the hall and the rooms beyond until the complete fireplace had been introduced; elsewhere, the open hearth was normally succeeded by a smoke hood projecting from a solid wall which was usually of stone.

The dates of the various improvements varied with the size-type of the house and, to some extent, with its location. In Surrey, smoke bays were being introduced in Small Houses during the second half of the 16C. and the early 17C. Fireplaces were introduced shortly afterwards but mainly in the early and mid 17C. In the north and west most surviving Small Houses, which are often no earlier than the late 17C., had smoke hoods, and fireplaces were not introduced into the main living room until the late 18C. or early 19C.

Staircases

Until the late 18C. the means of communication between the various floors of a multi-storey vernacular dwelling-house was virtually confined to variations of the straight flight ladder or the spiral staircase. Both were inconvenient in their separate ways but became gradually less cramped and awkward.

No doubt the simple ladder was once an essential ancillary to life in the simplest vernacular buildings, but, apart from the primitive 'croglofft' type cottages of Wales and Ireland, the form survives only in the straight flight stone staircases of some of the superior medieval houses and in the steep companion way framed up of treads and strings, or cut from roughly shaped timber baulks found in the inferior houses of the late 17C. and early 18C.

The vernacular counterpart of the stone spiral staircase of the medieval castle is usually found alongside a fireplace where its steeply tapered steps describe one half revolution in rising from one floor to the other. Quite often, and especially in the north-west, such a staircase was fitted into a projecting turret and, following an earlier architectural fashion, developed into a series of straight flights of solid stone or timber steps around a solid core.

From the late 17C. onwards, and gradually passing down the social scale, the framed timber staircase appeared in vernacular houses and was a prominent part of the 'double pile' plan. Such a staircase could be framed with 'newels', each newel post helping to make the transition between the various angles turned by the staircase as it rose, or it could be 'geometrical', employing even more skilful joinery to eliminate the heavy newels. However, the so-called 'dog-leg' staircase of stone or heavy timber, remained popular in Small Houses until well into the 19C.

Most vernacular houses had only one staircase, except that when an open hall separated two wings, each would have its own staircase and, especially in farm-houses of the late 18C. and early 19C., a separate service staircase was sometimes provided to help isolate family from servants.

Except when needed for defensive purposes, external staircases were rarely used to give access to upper storeys. When found in farm-houses, they usually served a granary or other storeroom rather than the domestic quarters.

a. The simple ladder and the slightly more elaborate companion way are illustrated. The latter was often fitted into a shallow cupboard at one end of the partition which separated the private rooms from the living-room.

b. The spiral staircase could be made either of separate stone steps cantilevered from the walls and meeting in a central vertical newel, or they could be of solid timber steps spanning between a timber wall and a mast-like newel.

c. Towards the end of the 16C., Large Houses began to have staircases consisting of straight flights of solid stone or timber steps rising around a solid stone or brick core. These were more convenient than the spiral staircase but gave no opportunity for display.

d. The framed newel staircase came into common use about the middle of the 17C. and both the newel posts, and the balusters encouraged elaborate carving well displayed in the open well.

e. In the smaller houses the dog-leg staircase had many of the advantages of the newel staircase but was easier to construct and more compact. In the double-pile plan the half-landing encouraged invention in window design.

4. ARCHITECTURAL DETAILS

Few vernacular buildings and very few examples of domestic vernacular are entirely without architectural adornment. The architectural details chosen may be inappropriate, the proportions unhappy, and the execution crude, but the intention—to extend the process of architectural design to the level of detail—was patently there.

To judge from surviving examples, the aim was to follow national fashion, and each change in fashion displayed on the supra-vernacular buildings of the capital or the great provincial centres was eventually followed at the vernacular level. But as a result of the time lag caused by slow communications and the natural caution and conservatism of vernacular designers, an innovation would often be introduced into a remote village long after it had passed out of use in fashionable society. The time lag diminished as communications improved, but it was never entirely eliminated. As a result of the varying characteristics of different building materials, the national fashions tended to develop regional variations. Thus, in a region of half-timbered building, nationally developed stone mouldings would be modified for use in timber and so help to develop a sub-style, or, in a region of hard, intractable stone, the mouldings developed nationally by skilled masons working in selected materials were adapted locally to the materials and skills available. Only in those regions where the available materials could permit absolutely no adornment, or poverty was so complete that only the barest essentials of buildings could be financed, would architectural details be absent.

Even in a single house there was a gradation in the quality of materials and details from the front, to the sides, and then to the rear of the building. Thus the windows on the front of an 18C. Lancashire farm-house might have double hung sashes in moulded stone architraves, the sides having horizontally sliding sashes in the jambs of a squared rubble wall, while on the rear wall re-used stone mullioned windows with timber casements would be set in random rubble. Similarly in a farmstead of one build, stable, barn, and granary would normally have the type of window and mouldings which had recently been abandoned for domestic use, while the cow-house, pig-sty etc., having lower status, would have unglazed openings following an even earlier pattern.

Towards the end of the vernacular period the resources of the local designer were extended by use of the newly available pattern books. With the aid of such a primer an up-to-date elevation could be designed and given appropriate details even if the sides and rear of a house followed the vernacular version of earlier architectural fashions. The pattern books usually indicated windows and doors as shaded voids; these were often provided in the vernacular elevation and glazed or not as internal arrangements suggested; the Window Taxes have been unjustly blamed for careless application of the rules from a pattern book.

There is no doubt that a good deal of local imitation took place, building contracts sometimes refer to one house which was being used as a model for another, and equally, there is little doubt that a craftsman, having adopted or devised a particular detail used it at every opportunity within the radius of his operations.

The evidence of architectural details ranks with documentary evidence in dating vernacular buildings. Reference to the authoritative architectural textbooks will help in using this evidence for dating, but one must always remember that these books have established dating criteria based on the use of architectural details in the most advanced and expensive buildings in the country and when making use of these criteria the time lag, itself varying with period and location, between initial appearance at national level, and final use in the remotest vernacular building was a very long one, measured in centuries rather than years in extreme instances. It is to be hoped that before long enough research will have been done with the aid of dated vernacular buildings for a full series of corrected time scales to be available for use in various parts of the country.

Windows and Doors Generally

Three stages in the continuous development of the window are distinguished here; they have been given the convenient, though only partially appropriate, names of medieval, sub-medieval, and renaissance. In each phase a distinction has been made between the overall shape of the window opening, the mouldings associated with it, and the provision for glazing and ventilation.

The three stages relate to the changes in sectional form of the domestic interiors which the windows were intended to serve. In the medieval hall house, tall windows with a few narrow lights were needed for the main hall or the solar, both rooms being open to the roof. But in the storied late medieval house, and in the Small Houses which were coming into the vernacular zone, rooms were low and usually ceiled and so horizontal runs of mullioned windows became the most appropriate type. By the early part of the 17C. the tall windows of the Italian Renaissance had begun their long period of influence. At first, rooms remained low in vernacular buildings and so the long horizontal run of the medieval window was replaced by two or three short square windows, but gradually tall rooms came into use and with them the tall renaissance window shape.

In most stone-bearing districts, some attempt was made to employ fashionable mouldings around the window openings. Where brick or an inferior stone was used for walling, superior stone was often carried from a quarry in an adjacent district in order to permit these mouldings.

The earliest surviving vernacular buildings appear to make no provision for glazing, and, indeed, it seems unlikely that glazed windows became common before the late 16C. in Large Houses or the late 17C. in Small Houses. But, as the early lattices of glass quarries in a network of lead cames required no structural preparation other than the provision of a few bars to which the lattices could be tied, it is difficult to decide if any specific example of a window of such a period was actually glazed. Early glass was cut from blown discs and is usually very thin and heavily marked. Later glass, from disc or cylinder was set in thick wooden glazing bars; these were gradually reduced in thickness until the early 19C., when, becoming almost too thin for stability, they were sometimes replaced by glazing bars of iron. Cheap but good quality sheet glass, available after about 1840, meant that most glazing bars could be omitted, and many earlier window frames were adapted for these large panes with unfortunate results for the scale of the building.

Three stages in the continuous development of the doorway have also been distinguished and they compare roughly in period with those suggested for the window. In each stage the shape of the door, the nature of any associated mouldings, and the form of the door itself have been separately considered.

As the doorway in a vernacular building was almost invariably related directly to human size and rarely depended on the needs of extravagant display there was little variation in the basic size and shape. However there were variations in width which are not easy to explain and the basic shape permitted a wide variety in the form of the head of the doorway.

In most stone-bearing districts the doorway was the point of concentration for such carving as the nature of the material, the wealth of the owner, and the skill of the mason would permit. This detail included the mouldings of the door jambs and the various embellishments—drip courses, shields, carved mottoes, pediments, swags etc.—which were demanded by changing architectural fashion. In districts of timber frame construction, and in those stone-bearing districts where the material was unsuitable for carving, the doorway was often framed out of heavy timber sections displaying an adaptation of the mason's mouldings.

There was a continuous improvement in the construction of the door and its method of hanging. Early doors were made of heavy vertical planks, battened at the rear and harr-hung on vertical wooden pins or hung by heavy strap hinges from brackets set in the jambs of the doorway. Later the door construction became lighter, and the door might be hung or hinged to a frame. Eventually the panelled door became available and this was hung on concealed hinges in the type of slender frame with which we are now familiar.

Some token acknowledgment is made of the wealth of fashionable architectural adornment displayed both on the exterior and the interior of quite humble dwelling-houses. These range from bays, porches, and other projections from the face of the building, to the simple panelling and ingeniously stopped mouldings which so often decorate the living-room of the most severe looking farm-house.

Windows: The Medieval Phase

Illustrated here are window forms originating in the medieval period but continuing, at the vernacular levels, almost until the 18C. There appear to be two main variations: the horizontal which was based on a series of vertical lancet type lights, and the horizontal which was based on a series of diamond-mullioned divisions of a wooden window frame. But both probably derive from the more commonly accepted medieval window shape of a vertical in stone or timber.

The stone-mullioned versions may run from between two and sixteen lights in one horizontal range, but the long runs are usually subdivided by king mullions into groups of three or four lights. In later examples, the windows were made taller with mullions steadied by transoms to give a rectangular shape more appropriate to the sub-medieval phase.

Mouldings in stone-mullioned windows followed the fashions set earlier at higher architectural levels. Wood-mullioned windows were normally square-cut bars set diagonally with narrow intermediate bars, but they could also be more or less direct copies of stone forms in the cheaper material. Windows were linked and protected by horizontal label or drip moulds.

During the earlier part of the phase, glazing was unusual, even for quite superior houses. Some examples survive of the hinged or sliding shutters which provided security and draught protection. A few examples also survive of the early lattices wired to the bars of wood-mullioned windows or to iron bars in stone-mullioned windows, but most have been replaced by later sashes.

Windows in half-timbered buildings followed these same general lines but usually with flimsier sections and more spindly details.

126

a. lancet with cusped head.

b. lancet with square head.

c. transomed window with cusped lights and spandrel at the head; designed for a rectangular opening; would normally have a 'drip' or 'label' mould above.

d. a squarish opening mullioned and transomed to give six lights each with three-centred arched heads.

e. wooden window frame with single diamond mullion.

f. range of five lights in a wooden frame with diamond mullion and intermediate vertical bars.

g. three-light window with ogee-arched heads and cusped spandrels, all of slender section appropriate to a timber-framed wall.

h. three-light window, square headed, and with splayed stone mullions.

i. six-light window, square headed, and with a king mullion and depressed beyond a separate splayed moulding.

j. splayed mullion and jamb. k. cavetto mullion and jamb. l. ovolo-moulded mullion and jamb. m. diamond mullion, square cut jamb. n. as before but with intermediate vertical bar. o. iron barred window (no glazing). p. horizontally sliding internal shutter; q. side hung internal shutters. r. glass quarries in lead came. s. lattice wired to horizontal iron bar; square and diamond panes shown.

Windows: The Sub-medieval Phase

The sub-medieval phase was a transition between the earlier period of long horizontal runs of narrow mullioned lights and the later period of tall balanced sash windows. It lasted in minor domestic work certainly until the mid-18C. and for workshops etc., until the mid-19C.

The characteristic window shape in this period was square. In stone districts the square shape was divided into two by a mullion, but often this has been removed to allow a new window frame to be inserted; where it survives the mullion may be thin, square-cut, set-back, and unrelated to any mouldings which surround the window. In brick districts the square or slightly elongated window would be set beneath a shallow arch and either divided by thin wooden mullions within the window frame into two or three lights, or filled with an overall network of horizontal and vertical glazing bars. In timber framed work, the window frames were of fairly heavy sections, often flush with, or even projecting slightly from the various cladding materials, tiles, plaster etc. which had come into use.

At this stage some form of ventilation by opening lights had become normal. In stone districts this took the form either of side hung opening casements in wrought iron or wood, or of horizontally sliding sashes. This latter form, the so-called Yorkshire sliding sash, was the inferior equivalent of the superior vertically sliding sash, but with its one fixed and one sliding portion, was particularly appropriate to the square window shape. In brick and timber frame districts, side hung casements were more common. In all districts at this period, the humbler buildings might be ventilated by no more than a single small opening light in a window of otherwise entirely fixed glazing.

a. square opening of two lights with vertical bars.
b. square two-light opening, one side-hung wooden casement, single horizontal wooden glazing bars.
c. as b. but with 'Yorkshire' horizontally sliding sash.
d. as b. but small panes under brick arch.
e. three-light window, wooden frames, centre light a side-hung casement, all under a shallow brick arch.
f. two-light window with square-cut stone mullion, wrought-iron frames, one side-hung one fixed, small panes.
g. as f. but in one square opening.
h. fixed window of small panes in wooden frame and with one small opening pane.

i. square-cut mullion and jamb adapted for glazing by lattices applied from the outside. j. chamfered mullion and jamb adapted for inside glazing. k. square-cut mullion set back from chamfered window opening. l. as k. but window has simple architrave surround. m. wrought-iron side-hung casement. n. wooden side-hung casement. o. wooden horizontally sliding sash.

Windows: The Renaissance Phase

The period characterized by the vertical window shape began at the higher vernacular levels towards the end of the 17C. and continued until the end of the vernacular tradition 200 years later. It included the Georgian window as normally understood together with the detailed variations introduced as part of the Greek and Gothic Revivals.

Although the basic shape was that of a vertical rectangle, lighting requirements sometimes led to variations. The most decorative of these was the Palladian or Gibbs window which was very popular for staircase landings; to provide more light into a living-room the basic window was widened, two hollow mullions containing counter balances for the sashes; in the North of England, where the mullioned tradition was never entirely lost, two vertical windows were added together to give a square shape. For Gothic Revival purposes the head of the vertical window was rounded or pointed, or two windows were collected beneath a label mould.

Mouldings were dominated by the standard renaissance forms, except in brick buildings. There, interest was concentrated on head and sill. At the window head the lintels were based on flat arches of gauged brickwork or had Gibbs-type details in stone, sometimes a single stone lintel being cut in imitation of separate voussoirs.

Early examples of the renaissance type window had stone or wood mullions and transomes with side hung opening casements, but few of these survive as they were soon superseded by the vertically sliding sash window developed in the late 17C. and early 18C. In vernacular examples the upper sash was originally fixed, the lower sliding in grooves and held by wedges or balanced by weights. Later in the 18C., the familiar balanced sash came into universal use.

a. window proportions: double square for window opening and 'side and diagonal' for individual panes.

b. hybrid with stone mullions and raised head to central light, quite commonly found in the Pennines.

c. 'Palladion' or 'Gibbs' window, central arched light and narrower square-headed lights at each side.

d. late 17C. type with mullion and transome of stone or timber and with side-hung opening light, wooden or of wrought iron.

e. 'Gothick' tracery in semi-circular head, a common staircase window.

f. Gothic Revival arched head.

g. Two-light square-headed Gothic Revival window under label mould, vertically sliding sashes without glazing bars.

h. Upper sash fixed, shown with heavy wooden glazing bars and with shallow reveals and wooden architrave as in timber framed wall.

i. Balanced sashes in brick wall.

j. Balanced sashes in deep reveal in stone wall.

k. Detail of fixed upper sash, note absence of parting bead and weights.

l. Balanced sashes.

m. Details of Victorian modification with drooping 'horns'.

131

Doors and Doorways: The Medieval Phase

During this period the most characteristic doorway at the vernacular level included the frameless door; the actual door being hinged direct to the structure of stone or wood rather than being hung on a door frame. Nevertheless in some parts e.g. the West Country and Wales a heavy door frame set into a stone opening was used.

The characteristic shape of the doorway depends on the width and the form of the head. Usually the doorway was the 2 ft. 10 ins. or 3 ft. width we would expect at the present day, but there are a number of examples, especially in the West of England, where the door is much wider than normal; these may possibly be related to use of the doors by wide-horned cattle as well as humans, or, it has been suggested, even designed for milk maids carrying two pails on a yoke! The form of the head includes variations on the arch, two-centred, three-centred, four-centred etc., following, with appropriate time lag, the general architectural fashion.

Mouldings on doors resembled those on windows except that the termination of a moulding at the base of a door jamb gave opportunity for variations in the design of a stop similar to the stopped mouldings of ceiling beams. Moulded drip courses, following the line of arched heads, or horizontal with dropped and returned ends, were used towards the end of the phase, but decorated lintels were uncommon.

Some examples of the original door survive. These are usually massive, consist of heavy ledges and planks or two layers of battens placed alternately, are usually studded with the ends of iron or wooden pegs, and are usually strong enough to give a defensive capability enhanced by a heavy drawbar. But carved and applied Gothic decoration is equally characteristic of the phase. In earlier examples, or in remote parts of the country an additional wrought iron grille was provided.

a. arched doorway in stone wall, splayed moulding to jamb and arch, drip mould terminating in carved corbels, wooden vertically planked door with studs, set in rebate in stone.

b. two-centred arch.

c. ogee arch.

d. three-centred arch.

e. four-centred arch.

f. moulded jamb and label, early 14C. type.

g. as f. but early 16C. type.

h. as f. but early 17C. type.

i. door of vertical planks and horizontal battens connected with wooden pegs, the innermost plank has been thickened and shaped to provide pegs for 'harr' hanging into a wooden socket at the top and an iron shoe at the bottom.

j. door knocker.

k. plank and batten door, iron pegs and moulded cover strips.

l. alternate plank and batten door, closely spaced wooden pegs.

m. wrought iron hinge used to hang the door on iron brackets built into the stone door jamb.

n. wrought iron gate used as inner defence, like a portcullis but side hung.

Doors and Doorways:
The Sub-medieval Phase

Roughly corresponding with the period of vernacular window design here called sub-medieval, there was a phase of doorway design which was neither medieval nor renaissance in substance but which included elements of both phases. In many parts of the country most of the surviving vernacular houses have doorways with the characteristics of this phase, including at one extreme, crude developments of Gothic precedent, and at the other, untutored introductions to the Renaissance.

In the stone bearing districts of the Pennines and extending westwards into the Lake District the most characteristic detail is the decorated lintel. No two examples are exactly alike, but one common form has a single lintel shaped at the base into a flat suggestion of a four-centred arch, decorated on the face with various combinations of initials and dates, and set below a simple dropped label mould; another, equally common, has the splayed or moulded jamb of the doorway carried up into the lintel to give a battlemented or false arched effect. Towards the end of the phase the mouldings took on a crude classical form and the label mould was simplified into a cornice-like shape. Where a heavy wooden door frame was provided, this was sometimes quite heavily moulded, or had a shaped head, presenting an exotic, almost oriental, combination of curves and angles.

Heavy wooden doors continued to be hung from brackets in the door jamb and secured by a drawbar, but in later examples, simple framed doors came into use, hinged to the door frame, and equipped with clumsy, though sometimes well-decorated, locks.

a. doorway with a false four-centred arched head (straight sides to pointed head) in a splayed jamb, deep lintel with carved device, label mould with dropped and returned ends, the door is shown open to reveal a drawbar socket.

b. false four-centred arch.

c. heavy wooden frame.

d. moulded square-headed opening.

e. carved head framed into heavy wooden door frame.

f. and *g*. two examples of decorated lintel.

h. chamfered jamb and label mould late 17C. type.

i. moulded jamb and cornice early 18C. type.

j. wrought iron strap hinge.

k. door of planks and battens with concealed hinges in heavy wooden frame.

Doors and Doorways: Renaissance and Revival Phase

During this phase the emphasis of the doorway as the point of concentration of interest and decoration in the centre of an elevation reached its culmination. Even in the plain, utilitarian design of a terraced cottage, few doorways were without some form of pediment or canopy.

As well as the normal square head, semi-circular and elliptical heads were adopted, and, during the revival phase, the arched head returned to fashion. These variations depended to some extent on the development of the fanlight to introduce daylight into the lobby or 'hall' into which the front door now opened in all but the poorest houses. The square head, however, was modified by the use of voussoirs, or a flat brick arch, or a decorated keystone, to provide a decorative effect.

The conventional door surround in this phase included a pediment, triangular or segmental, together with moulded architraves, and a good deal of detailed variation was made even within the standardized form. Where the type of stone permitted, initials, date and a motto were sometimes incised.

With the improvement in joinery techniques the doors during this phase usually had four or six raised and fielded panels and bolection moulds. The panels could move within the grooves of their frames, the raised and fielded effect gave shape and substance to the panel, while the bolection moulding embraced the joint between the body of the door and the panels but concealed movement between them.

a. a type of door and doorway found, at the vernacular level from the middle of the 18C. onwards. The stone architrave and head with heavily emphasized but quite false keystone show reasonably faithful imitation of classical precedent. The door is framed and panelled and set in a separate light timber frame or casing.

b. triangular pediment.

c. segmental pediment.

d. scroll type pediment.

e. broken pediment.

f. semi-circular arch with keystone.

g. stepped voussoirs (usually carved out of a single stone lintel).

h. flat hood or cornice.

i. simple architraves with date panel.

j. bolection moulded architrave, late 17C. to mid 18C.

k. architrave and cornice with pulvinated frieze, mid to late 18C.

l. simple chamfered architrave with Greek Revival cornice, early 19C.

m. framed wooden door of six panels showing mouldings and raised panel.

n. details of bolection moulding and the H and L type hinges used especially on internal doors.

137

Architectural Details: Other External Ornament

It is quite impossible to give more than a token representation to the minor architectural details in which the vernacular designers displayed their ingenuity, and since so many buildings of this class present no more than the bare bones of peasant building techniques for inspection it would, perhaps, be inappropriate to emphasize the few which came closest to the conventions of polite architecture. Nevertheless three categories of ornament are mentioned here: bay windows, porches, and decorative details.

Bay windows, popular in the superior buildings of the medieval period, returned to favour, in both bold and shallow projection, during the Regency. Oriels had no comparable successors except in the seaside towns where such projecting windows could give a view of the sea and ships. Galleries of various sorts were occasionally found in vernacular buildings, especially when the lie of the land entailed building on several levels. Balconies and verandahs were found towards the end of the period of vernacular building and were an unusual feature adopted for development by the clever designers of the Vernacular Revival movement.

At the vernacular level, porches seem to have come into favour towards the end of the 16C., possibly as a last token of the former dignity of a defensive tower, or possibly as a remote acknowledgement of the form of the classical portico. Apart from its use as a means of reducing draughts through the main doorway, the porch also gave an opportunity for display of the limited extravagance of vernacular detail. Smaller, single-storey porches were surprisingly uncommon, even in exposed upland situations.

138

a. oriel window from timber framed building, carved solid bracket (late 16C.).

b. square-cut bay window (early 17C.).

c. bow window (early 19C.).

d. splayed bay window (late 18C.).

e. spinning gallery (late 17C.).

f. balcony of wrought iron (late 18C.-early 19C.).

g. two-storey porch with rose window (mid 17C.).

h. multi storey porch with carved plaque and niche for statue (late 16C.).

i. open single-storey porch (late 16C.).

j. closed single-storey porch (mid 18C.).

k. barge boards with finials, pierced decoration and pendants.

l. lead rain water head with initials and date.

m. fire mark.

n. date plaque, raised lettering.

o. date plaque, incised lettering.

p. date plaque, deeply incised lettering.

q. date plaque, recessed base leaving bold raised lettering.

r. lettering in stone set in flint.

s. bow window used in shops in early 19C.

t. sundial.

139

Architectural Details: Internal Ornament

In spite of the many modifications which most vernacular buildings have suffered in order to make them more comfortable or, more recently, to help them match the suburban image of the ideal home of the women's magazine, there is a quite substantial survival of internal architectural details. Of the wealth of regional variation over the course of time, three groups of detail have been selected for comment: partitions, built-in cupboards, and moulded ceiling beams.

Many of the common plan forms adopted by the vernacular house designers made use of a partition to separate private rooms from the main living-room. These were usually non-structural and could conveniently be made of timber whatever the material of the main walls of the house. The most common type of partition has been given the name of 'muntin and plank'. It consisted of alternate thick and thin planks, the latter set in grooves running vertically along the edges of the former. The muntins, in superior examples were moulded on the living-room side, while the planks might be given some simplified version of the linenfold pattern. Later these and other internal partitions were framed of studs and rails with square panels between and with light renaissance mouldings for decoration.

During the later 17C., built-in cupboards were popular in farm-houses. The larger cupboards were sometimes built into the timber partitions, while the smaller cupboards included the so-called spice cupboard, set into the fireplace wall, and generally assumed to be the dry depository of valuable salt and spices.

When the open hall passed out of favour, the architectural invention which had been devoted to the cusping and other ornament of roof timbers was diverted in part to the moulding of the heavy beams which carried the intermediate floor. The simple chamfered beam was the basis of many varieties of moulding and stop.

a. part of a partition between living-room and private rooms showing muntin and plank partition framed between beam and cill and incorporating a doorway. Many examples survive dating from late 15C. to late 17C.

b. these partitions sometimes incorporated a built-in bench with shaped pew-like ends.

c. from about the middle of the 17C. framed partitions were used in vernacular buildings; the example incorporates a framed door.

d. detail of a muntin and plank partition; there were several variations, the one illustrated has thick planks chamfered to slide into grooves in the muntins.

e. detail of early framed partitioning; later examples used mitred, or scribed joints to allow the mouldings to run around the panels.

f. detail of a built-in 'spice cupboard'. *g*. basic chamfer and stop. *h*. early 17C. moulding to a beam, ovolo flanked by cavettos. *i*. flat chamfer stopped by a quirk and a tongue, early 17C. *j*. ovolo stopped by tongue, late 16C. or early 17C. *k*. variation of j. with ovolo stopped before the tongue. *l*. bead type mould stopped by flat and tongue, mid 17C. *m*. flat chamfer with fillet and stop, mid 17C. *n*. flat chamfer with half pyramid stop, mid 17C. *o*. ovolo, fillet, and cavetto tapered stop, late 17C.

5. FARM BUILDINGS

Introduction

The association of the farm-house with roses round the door and ivy on the wall compares favourably with the manure underfoot and dust up above which are more commonly associated with the other buildings of the farmstead. Perhaps for this reason, as well as others more academic, the design and construction of farm buildings has received even less attention from scholars than the planning, choice of materials and architectural detailing of farm-houses. And yet the sheer volume of space enclosed, quite apart from the constructional problems presented by farm buildings should remind us that the expense and effort devoted to farm buildings has, for the past three centuries been greater than that devoted to farm-houses, while the architectural qualities of cathedral-like barns and elegant granaries are often superior to those of the farm-houses they served. No apology, therefore is made, for devoting a reasonable proportion of this handbook to farm buildings.

As the study of farm buildings is even further extended into infancy than the study of other branches of vernacular architecture, this chapter is even less well-founded on published research than the others. No comprehensive national study of the history of farm buildings has yet been published (though there are indications that regional studies may soon appear) nor have more than a handful of articles been devoted either to selected farmsteads or typical farm buildings. Nevertheless this chapter attempts to list briefly the characteristics of the farm buildings normally found in England and Wales, to note the arrangements commonly adopted in the layout of the farmstead, and to illustrate the effects of different farming practices and improved farming technology on the development of farm building design.

The surviving evidence from which the vernacular architecture of farm buildings can be studied covers an even shorter period than that relating to domestic vernacular architecture. Apart from the great medieval barns such as Bredon or Great Coxwell which are scarcely in the vernacular zone, few surviving agricultural buildings, stone or brick walled, appear to have been erected before the middle of the 17C. or, if timber framed, before the 16C. and the majority appear to be of late 18C. and early 19C. date. However, the vernacular content of farm buildings remained considerable until late in the 19C. and a terminal date of 1880 encompasses most of the examples worth study.

While the farming pattern of England and Wales gives a variety almost as complex as that of geology, for the present purposes there appear to have been three main types of farming practice which were significant: the predominantly arable cultivation of the eastern counties of England, the predominantly pastoral farming of the hilliest regions of Northern England, Central Wales and South-Western England, and the large area of mixed farming of the remainder of the country. Pastoral farming required virtually no buildings, arable farming required little more than capacious barns and sheds for the few loose cattle, but mixed farming required a considerable and increasing variety of buildings for the closely interrelated farming processes.

It is hard for the present day farmer, let alone the layman, to appreciate the importance of home-grown corn until late in the 19C. Oats, wheat and barley were essential for consumption by the farmer and his family, while oats at least were a vital part of the diet of his animals. Straw was essential for bedding and the conversion of manure into fertilizer for return to the land, while in most parts of the country it was the normal roofing material. But as yields were low harvesting difficult and the proportion to be retained for seed was high, much cultivable land had to be devoted to cereals. For the temporary storage and conversion of the cereal crop, one or more barns were required on every farmstead, and this building is the one most commonly found, and usually the one most ancient on the typical farmstead. However, changes in animal husbandry, the greater use of root crops and vegetables both to improve the diet of the animals and maintain the fertility of the soil, and improvements in the method of threshing and winnowing meant that after the middle of the 19C. the barn as commonly understood had become obsolete, and the large scale imports first of prairie-grown corn and later of frozen meat has led to the elimination of the barn as a building type.

Because the arable land was so vital to farming operations over most of the country, the power source which permitted cultivation of this land was equally vital. Until comparatively recent times the power for plough, harrow, and cart was provided by the ox, and as not all farmers could field a complete team, systems of common cultivation depended on the contribution of one or two healthy members from each participant. Similarly, the milking cow and her butter and cheese were so important, especially during the winter months that a house for the accommodation of cow and ox is found on most farmsteads. Where associated with the dwelling house in the 'long house' and similar arrangements, the significance of the cow-house as a building type becomes even more clear.

The horse has often been considered second only to man in the kingdom of mammals, and his accommodation has been given almost as much attention in early times. But in most parts of the country use of the horse was restricted to carriage, pack, and riding, it being considered too valuable an animal, and too expensive to keep, to replace the ox for general farm purposes. Even when the horse became, during the later 18C., the principal draught animal, the farm horses were separately housed from the carriage and riding horses. Both, however, required stables and this building type was commonly found on the farmstead from about 1750 onwards.

With the virtual elimination of the horse by the tractor since about 1950 few stables remain in use, but conversion to other uses has rarely obliterated all evidence of their original design.

The edible or marketable produce so dearly won from the land was for a long time carefully guarded within the dwelling house. But improvements in farming methods and increased productivity generally from the middle of the 18C. onwards meant that a specific building in the form of a granary was designed for the accommodation of threshed grain and, perhaps, ground flour and bran. At the same time the increasing range of wheeled implements and carts available to the farmer and required for improved cultivation led to the demand for a cart and implement shed. As the cart shed had to be at ground level, while the granary was best placed at the upper level, the combined granary/cart shed was provided on most farmsteads in mixed farming areas from the late 18C. onwards.

While the especially valuable and particularly vulnerable cattle were kept in a cow house, in most parts of the country the young stock were folded in the farmyard during the winter. There they were contained and protected by other farm buildings, but the shelter shed was developed as a building type to provide some shelter from the weather when feeding. In some parts of the South West, this was combined with hay storage to form the two-storied linhay. The open sided haybarn was developed in other parts of the country for the accommodation of such of the hay crop as could not be housed in the lofts over cow-house and stable. In districts with a more severe climate, hay was enclosed in a barn similar in form to the corn barn, and this was often located in the fields distant from the farm-house where combined accommodation for hay and young cattle took the form of the field-barn. Amongst the other minor buildings of the farmyard may be mentioned the pigsty and the dovecot, the one sometimes incorporating a hen-house and the other, occasionally surviving from more aristocratic days as an independent structure but more commonly incorporated with barn or even granary.

Some farmsteads also incorporate minor industrial buildings in the form of various kilns. The best known is the oast-house of South Eastern

England, but corn-drying kilns were formerly equally common in the wet high lying districts of England and Wales, where late and poor cereal crops had to be harvested damp or not at all. In barley growing districts, a malting kiln is sometimes found, while in districts with limestone out-crop, lime kilns dating from the late 18C. may be seen, usually in the fields, rather than as part of the farmstead.

Thus the barn, cow-house, stable, granary, cart shed and other minor buildings combined with the farmyard to form the working part of the farmstead as a whole. These buildings were, of course, lower in status than those of the domestic part of the economy and within this lower rank had their own grades of quality. Pride of place was normally granted to the great corn barn, though the stable might be given more careful archi-tectural adornment, while pig-sty and kiln were the most utilitarian. In construction they followed, normally, the local patterns set by domestic buildings, though with an appreciably longer time lag for the adoption of new materials: many a set of timber framed and thatch-roofed farm buildings, for instance, lies alongside a brick and tiled farm-house. In architectural detailing, similarly, they lag behind: the granary for instance being provided with wood mullioned and shuttered unglazed windows at a time when even the humblest part of the farm-house had glazed casements.

The need for recording and study of farm buildings is even more urgent than the need for study of houses. Most houses can be adapted or extended to meet a changing way of domestic life; the drift of permanent settlement from the countryside is to some extent counteracted by the enthusiasm for weekend cottages. But there is scarcely a single traditional farm building type which can be employed or even adapted to con-temporary farming methods. The barn has been obsolete for a century, the traditional cow-house is unhygienic for milk production and unsuitable for labour-saving methods of feeding and care. The stable has been obsolete since the tractor superseded the horse. Neither granary nor cart shed are needed. The silage pit has replaced the Dutch Barn; the pig fattening factory has replaced the pig-sty. Farmers and landowners have, in many cases, maintained obsolete farm buildings which they know to be uneconomical; but stone tile will not be replaced much longer and stone walls will eventually crumble; the multi-purpose steel and asbestos shed will replace the farmyard and its attendant buildings. The process is in its early stages, but before long the evidence will disappear; before it does so, it is imperative that the buildings be recorded, their story unravelled and forgotten farming processes recalled, and significant examples defined for preservation.

Farm Buildings: Location and Layout

Before examination of the individual building of the farmstead, the location and layout may be of interest.

Most farmsteads will be located either in nucleated settlements (villages), in groups of two or three (hamlets), or will be isolated. The nucleated settlements survive from periods of common cultivation on the open field or related systems of agriculture. Farms located in villages will be the few survivors of the many, large and small, which made up the community. Farmsteads located in hamlets or as part of very tiny groups are normally associated with pastoral farming, or mixed farming with a high pastoral element—there are few villages but many hamlets in mountainous Wales. But such farmsteads in other districts may be the survivors of a former nucleated village which has become otherwise deserted and decayed. Isolated farmsteads usually represent occupation of waste land which may have occurred at any time: medieval clearance of wooded land, or occupation of uncultivated moor; Elizabethan colonization of the upper slopes of valley sides, or 19C. enclosure of common land with new farmsteads established in the centre of a compact group of square fields. Other evidence is essential before the full implication of farmstead location may be understood.

The layout or pattern of the farmstead has been a source of fascination; between the extremes of the scattered building of the hill farming peasant and the carefully marshalled ranks of the 'model farmery' various attempts at classification have been made. A simple broad distinction is suggested here, but a great deal of work remains to be done before we understand such meaning as there may be in the shape of the farmstead.

146

Some farmstead locations: *a*. nucleated village, surviving farmsteads numbered; *b*. hamlet in fields of ancient enclosure, three farmsteads indicated; *c*. isolated farmstead in fields of recent enclosure.

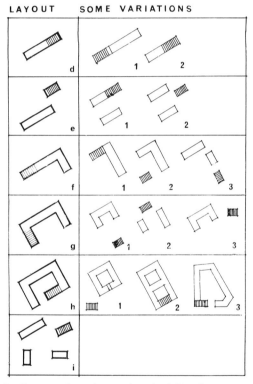

LAYOUT   SOME VARIATIONS

Some farmstead layouts (the hatched portion represents the farmhouse).

d. Elongated.—variation 1 indicates a 'longhouse' house and cow house interconnected, 2 indicates a laithe house of one build but not interconnected.

e. Parallel—variation 1 has a connected and 2 a separated farmhouse.

f. L-shaped—the three variations differ mainly in the position of the farmhouse.

g. U-shaped—among variations 1 shows a separate farmhouse axially related to the farm buildings, 3 a farmhouse quite detached and distinct.

h. Courtyard—1 has a detached farmhouse, 2 a farmhouse incorporated in one of the yards, 3 an irregular courtyard resulting from amalgamation of buildings. *i*. Scattered—especially in mountain farmsteads, different periods of build as well as difficult sites lead to disorderly development.

147

Farm Buildings: Combination Arrangements

One of the devices employed in design of farm buildings at the present day is the combination of all or most of the activities of the farmstead under one roof. Like so many of the inspirations of modern designers it is, in fact a resurrection of a former practice. Two examples of the practice are illustrated here.

The huge steeply pitched roof enfolding house and farm buildings is still a dominant feature of the rural landscape in Denmark and North Germany. It is more than likely that such combined buildings were erected in those parts of England which came under Danish influence after the Dark Ages, and the medieval domestic aisled hall may be a remnant of such a traditional form. No such combined dwelling and set of farm building survives intact and on such a scale, but there is an echo of the arrangement in some of the larger 18C. barns in which cow-houses, loose boxes, and shelter sheds are enclosed between the projecting porches and covered by the extended roof of a threshing barn.

An extremely compact combination farm building is the Bank Barn of the English Lake District. Here a natural or artificial slope is essential; from the lower level there is access to a cart shed flanked by cow-houses and stable, while at the upper level, a ramp, on the opposite side of the building, leads to a conventional barn. Hatches enable fodder to be dropped from barn to manger, and an economical building form was equally economical in labour. The origin of the Bank Barn is obscure and the many examples are, in England and Wales, confined almost entirely to parts of the Lake Counties, but similar buildings are found in Switzerland and Pennsylvania.

a. Combination barn, cow house, and stable, isometric. *b.* plan.

c. Typical Lake District Bank Barn in cutaway isometric showing threshing floor (1), winnowing door (2), cow house (3).

d. View from the lower slope showing the doors to cart shed and stable.

149

Farm Buildings:
The Barn for Hand Threshing

The barn is normally considered as a warehouse; a place in which crops were stored; but most surviving barns are more properly considered as factories where raw materials were processed into finished products and stored only temporarily.

The process of hand threshing with flail, which was universal until the mid-19C., and which has only recently passed finally out of use, required that the sheaves of unthreshed corn be stacked on one side of the threshing floor, while threshed straw was stacked on the other side. Day by day throughout the winter, sheaves were opened onto the floor, beaten by the flails of the two-man threshing team, the straw residue lifted to one side, and the ears winnowed by natural draught between two doors. The process was necessarily a slow and laborious one, but it provided fodder and litter as it was needed by the animals, and it provided employment for the labourers when they could not work in the fields.

The process of hand threshing governed the basic design of the barn which is illustrated here.

Variations on the basic design arose through different farming practices and improved farming methods and several of the common variations are also illustrated.

a. Cutaway isometric showing threshing floor, storage bays for sheaves and straw, opposite doors for light and draught, low partition.
b. Single barn, one threshing floor.
c. Double barn, two floors.
d. Asymmetrical barn unequal bays.

e. Projecting porch extending threshing floor.
f. Cheeks protecting floor.
g. Canopy protecting floor and doors.
h. and i. Ventilation patterns in brick.
j. and k. Ventilators in stone.
l. Dovecot in gable of barn.
m. Weather boarded single aisled barn.
n. Barn aisled on all four sides.

Farm Buildings:
The Barn for Machine Threshing

Many attempts were made to improve upon the slow and costly process of hand threshing, especially as improved farming methods increased the yield of cereal crops. But it was not until 1786 that the invention by Andrew Meikle of a threshing machine began the elimination of the hand process. Simple hand-operated winnowing fans had been used, but from the early years of the 19C. improvements in the threshing machine enabled threshing, winnowing, and grading to be done in one operation.

The threshing machine required a lot of power and several sources were used: occasionally windmills provided power, more frequently water-mills, either from continuous supply or using water from a pond. On the largest farms a stationary steam engine provided ample power. But the most frequently used power source for threshing, and for the cutting and mixing machines which were simultaneously developed, was the horse engine. This could take two forms, the sweep, in which the horses stepped over the drive shaft, and the overhead gearing, in which the horses trod a circular route underneath a crown wheel and pinion gear serving a horizontal drive shaft. The former type was usually in the open air, and only a circular sinking or embankment will now show its position; the latter type was usually housed in a building, of which many still survive.

Later in the 19C., the portable steam engine taken, with the threshing machine, from farm to farm converted a slow daily process into a quick two or three day operation. The remaining stationary threshing machines were eventually converted to drive by oil or gas engine, but horse engines remained in use for the lighter cutting and mixing machinery.

a. The cutaway isometric shows a barn served by an external, sweep type horse engine. Four horses draw the engine which was connected to a threshing machine in one bay of the barn. There is a vestigial threshing floor with a winnowing door for emergency use. The remainder of the barn is occupied by a cow house with loft over.

b. The sketch shows a barn with a three-horse overhead type threshir.g machine. This was housed in a square-ended projection from the barn. *c., d., e.* Alternative forms of horse engine house; all show the ventilation openings needed; *e* is the type found in Northumberland and in Devon.

153

Farm Buildings: The Cow-House

The cow-house was required on most farms to accommodate the more valuable oxen and cattle in safety and protected from the worst of the weather. Variations appear to be mainly in provision for feeding and tying and development lay mainly in the improvement but eventual elimination of the loft as a store for fodder.

There appears to have been a difference in feeding practice within the country: in some parts a wide feeding passage ran across the cow-house and cattle were tethered nose on to the passage and tail on to the manure passages; in others cows were tethered nose towards the cross wall and tail on to a single manure passage, the fodder being brought to individual feeding boxes from behind. Similarly there were variations in tying: in some parts cows were tethered in pairs, a low timber, slate, or stone partition separating each pair; in other parts, they were tethered singly between light posts. There is insufficient information available at present to define the areas of each different practice.

It was usual for hay and sometimes straw to be stored in a loft over the cow-house, with a trapdoor and ladder giving access between the two levels. During the 18C. and early 19C. this loft space tended to increase in height until it became a full upper storey with a regular series of pitching eyes facing the yard.

Early cow-houses were low and dark with the little ventilation provided by the open upper part of a feeding passage door. Light and ventilation were considered detrimental. During the 19C. there was a change in practice, and cow-houses became larger, well lit and ventilated, open to the roof without loft and with separate feeding and manure passages running along the building.

154

a. Central feeding passage. *b*. Two feeding passages. *c*. Longitudinal feeding passage. *d*. Central longitudinal feeding passage. *e*. No feeding passage. *f*. Single tethering, no partitions. *g*. Double tethering, partitions. *h*. Cutaway isometric shows relationship between feeding passage, stalls, and loft. *i*. Low loft mainly in roof space. *j*. Timber framed loft wall. *k*. Tall loft with open side. *l*. Tall loft with pitching eyes. *m*. Cow-house with central longitudinal feeding passage and flanking manure passages added to one end of a barn. *n*. Small cow-house intended for cattle fed from behind.

Farm Buildings: Stables

Probably for reasons of status as much as anatomy, the horse was given taller, more spacious, and better lit accommodation than the cow or humble ox.

Each horse was given a separate stall with a substantial wooden partition long enough to prevent horses kicking each other and tall enough to prevent them biting each other. Often there would be a separate manger and feeding trough. On the smaller farms the stalls ran along the building, three horses being accommodated in the width of the building, but on the larger farms there were usually ranks of horses with stalls running across the building. In both cases a loose box for sick horse or foaling mare would be included.

Over the stable there was normally a loft containing hay. Access was by trap door and ladder from within the stable, and often a gap in the floor or a series of trap doors enabled hay to be dropped direct into each manger. Sometimes, the loft acted as a granary, hence the legends of carters piercing the floor to obtain extra oats for their horses. Sometimes also the loft acted as a barrack room for the carters, the horses serving as a source of heat.

Within the walls of the stable there were usually 'keeping holes' for grooming equipment while tackle was hung on the wall. On the larger farms, however, a separate but adjacent harness room was provided.

Since so few stables remain in use on farms it is sometimes difficult to distinguish the former stable. Usually the height and shape of the room, the height and width of the door, and the provision of windows act as clues, while a horse's shoe over the door should clinch the matter.

a. Stable with four stalls and a loose box.   *b.* Stable with five stalls and longitudinal manure passage.   *c.* Diagram showing a stall with its manger, trough, and partitions. *d.* Cutaway isometric showing the stalls and loft. *e.* Typical stable as for plan *a.* *f.* Stable with pitching eyes to loft. *g.* Simple stable and loft for one hackney pony. *h.* Elaborate stable and loft for several carriage and riding horses.

Farm Buildings: Granary/Cart Shed

As its name suggests, the granary was intended principally for the storage of grain which had been threshed but not milled. The grain was stored sometimes in chests but more commonly in heaps on the floor. It was believed that movement of air below the floor would help to keep the grain sweet, while, at first floor level, spoilage by rats could be reduced. The walls and ceiling were sometimes plastered, and the floor carefully boarded.

The cart shed was provided to protect the carts and farm machinery from the worst of the weather. The earlier timber jointed implements suffered from both rain and sunshine and covered accommodation was desirable. This usually took the form of an open fronted shed, though sometimes a draw through was provided in one bay. The cart shed might be a separate single-storey building but very often was combined with a first floor granary. Access to the granary was usually by an external staircase rising up the side of the cart shed but sometimes a front or internal staircase was installed.

There were two particular structural problems to this building type, one was the support of the granary wall over the open front of the cart shed, the other was the inconvenience of a tie beam below head height in the granary. The one problem was solved by the use of piers of stone, brick, or heavy timber posts, together with lintels or arches, the other led to the use of various roof trusses which omitted the tie beams, e.g. the post and pad.

a. Ground and first floor plans of a typical cart shed with granary over.
b. Cart shed with draw through. *c*. Cutaway isometric showing cart shed
and granary. *d*. Detail of post and pad truss; the tie beam being truncated
by a short post braced back to the floor beam. *e*. Granary/cart shed; stone
piers, external gable stairs. *f*. Two-bay granary/cart shed, re-used crucks
as lintels. *g*. Four-bay granary/cart shed, timber framed front wall, internal staircase. *h*. Three-bay granary/cart shed, external stair at front.
i. small granary raised on staddle stones, movable bridge from steps to
door. *j*. detail of two-piece staddle stone. *k*. large granary of one and a half
storeys raised over deep implement shed.

Farm Buildings: Shelter Shed

a. plan of free standing shelter shed.
b. plan of shelter shed attached to a wall.
c. cutaway isometric, showing half-trusses and colonnade.
d. beams carried on timber post.
e. beams carried on stone pier.
f. beams carried on cast iron column.

Where cattle were lodged in the farmyard during winter it became customary to provide an open-fronted shelter shed in which the cattle could be fed and also could shelter from the worst of the weather. Such a shed might be a separate building or back on to an existing wall. Timber or cast iron posts, brick piers, or stone columns have been used for the colonnade which supports the roof. Late 19C. and early 20C. developments included the transformation of the shelter shed into an entirely covered foldyard.

Farm Buildings: Linhay

a. plan of lower part of linhay.
b. isometric showing full height stone piers.
c. isometric showing timber posts at upper level.
d. cutaway isometric showing method of support of the loft floor.

In lowland Devon and occasionally elsewhere a more elaborate shelter was provided. This, called locally a linhay, consisted of an open fronted shelter on the ground floor with a hay loft (tallet) above. In earlier examples the loft was open fronted, but later weather board protection to the hay was provided.

Farm Buildings: Hay Barn

a. brick-wall, tiled roof, hay barn as found especially in Staffordshire, Cheshire and South Lancashire.

a

b

In mixed farming areas, especially in the Midlands, covered accommodation for the hay crop was sometimes provided in the form of a 'Dutch Barn'. For ease of access and benefit of ventilation the roof was carried on piers of stone or brick. The outer piers sometimes had 'Gothic' arches while the intermediate trusses might be carried by timber posts or, in later examples, by cast iron columns. *b*. Dutch style barns with rise and fall roofs were used in the 19C.

Farm Buildings: Field Barn

c. cutaway isometric showing the use of the slope, the 'sink mow' with hay swept in at high level and removed for consumption at low level, also loft over loose box for young cattle.

d. field barn across slope.

c

d

In upland districts greater protection was given to the hay. At the same time the practice developed in many areas of erecting a field barn on newly enclosed land, distant from the farmstead, and housing young cattle below and hay above. Such field barns are especially prominent in the Yorkshire Dales.

Farm Buildings: Pig-sty

a. a rather elaborate triple pig-sty with a hen house up above; feeding troughs are incorporated in the walls of the exercise yards.

Many farmsteads still include, but rarely utilize, a pig-sty. In the traditional arrangement the sty consisted of a covered portion and a walled yard. Often a loft served as a hen house with a ramped access plank; the yard sometimes incorporated an ingenious feeding trough.

Farm Buildings: Dovecot

b. a rectangular dovecot with nesting boxes in each wall and access for the birds through a sort of clearstorey.
c. octagonal dovecot.
d. cylindrical dovecot, cutaway diagram.

Before the improved feeding stuffs simplified the problem of fattening stock through winter, pigeons and doves were considered a useful source of fresh meat. Their manure was also highly valued. Dovecots were for long restricted to the gentry but later examples are found on large farms. They are usually either rectangular or are a variation on the cylinder. Access for the birds was usually through a lantern, while eggs were collected with the aid of a revolving ladder.

Farm Buildings: Corn drying kiln

a. In the cutaway isometric is shown a corn kiln used, it is assumed jointly, in hamlets in the Lake District. The grille was based on specially shaped pieces of slate.

b. Perforated tile often used for floor of drying chamber.

Corn drying kilns were formerly common in the wetter agricultural regions. Although eventually associated with the mills such kilns had previously been erected for individual farmsteads or small farming groups. The parts consisted of a drying chamber in which the damp corn was spread on a horse hair blanket over a grille of stone or slate slats, or directly on perforated tiles, and a heating chamber sometimes served by a chimney but more commonly without.

Farm Buildings: Oast House; Maltings

c. The diagram shows the type of oast house commonly found in Kent and Sussex.

d. Double cylindrical oast house

e Sketch of a small maltings.

The oast house was a kiln designed for drying hops. Most are circular and have a cowl over the vent and adjustable to the wind. Other examples are square.

6. URBAN VERNACULAR AND MINOR INDUSTRIAL BUILDINGS

The domestic vernacular of the countryside and the vernacular buildings of the farmstead are linked by a common dependence on agriculture. While such probably represent the majority of vernacular buildings and comprise those which are most picturesque and richest in regional variation, the vernacular field is also occupied by buildings linked in their dependence on commerce and industry—the urban houses of the medieval merchant and the Victorian artisan, and the buildings, both urban and rural, designed for primitive industrial processes. This chapter, therefore, brings together notes on a number of widely differing building types, mainly urban, from various periods, but dependent in some way on commerce and industry.

The design of the urban equivalents of the Large Houses, Small Houses, and Cottages of the countryside was governed like that of their rural counterparts by the functional demands on plan and sectional form, the limitations of available building materials, and the dictates of architectural fashion; but their design were also governed to a much more substantial extent by the problems of restricted sites and the regulations necessary for neighbourly design. Although few British towns developed within so tight a strait-jacket as most towns on the Continent, pressure on the most desirable land within a city boundary meant that plots had to be filled and volume gained by upward building during medieval and later times. When changes in commercial organization and improvements in transport, particularly during the 18C., led to an increase in the size of many towns this took the form of more intensive use of existing urban land—building on gardens for instance, as well as expansion of towns along the roads, and by formation of suburbs. But the vast transfer of population from country to town which took place during the 19C. was a result of the operation of industry of all kinds—mining, manufacturing, transporting—on an unprecedented scale.

a. Urban vernacular before the Industrial Revolution: Louth, Lincs.

b. Urban vernacular after the Industrial Revolution: Hyde, Cheshire.

Urban Vernacular: Medieval

In spite of the Roman origin so often claimed for the street pattern of any ancient town in which two streets cross at right angles, few towns retain an earlier layout than the medieval, and even then regular planning was probably exceptional the layout of most medieval English towns being dependent on local topography rather than on human foresight.

However, development based on a market place, a quayside, or a grid-iron pattern of streets can often be detected. The market place was often an elongated rectangle (e.g. St. Albans) but subsequent encroachment has, in many places, obscured the original shape. The quay side development may be seen at ancient ports such as Southampton, or Kings Lynn, where merchants' warehouses and domestic quarters lined the quay; but shifts in water channels and later urban developments have usually left the early quayside high and dry. Grid-iron development was characteristic of the many medieval New Towns (such as Salisbury, Winchelsea, and Conway) in which houses lined the rectangular streets, and churches or public spaces occupied island blocks left open for the purpose; but the many advantages of a grid-iron street pattern, especially in measurement, definition, and conveyance of land, led to its use in most towns from the medieval period almost to the present day.

Even when confined by a wall, a medieval town included a wide range of densities. The most important streets and the most valuable sites might be crowded, but the remainder of the town was occupied by separately walled enclosures, such as a monastery or cathedral close with a spacious setting to important buildings, or by individual houses, each set in a garden, much as they would be placed in a country village. Between and around the more permanent houses occupied by the wealthier landowners and tradesmen, were the simple and flimsy cottages of the poor, of which very few remains survive.

For this period, the most characteristic urban vernacular is represented by the houses of merchants and tradesmen of which quite substantial portions remain in use in many of our older towns.

a. In the centre of a typical medieval market town, the front of each long narrow plot of land would be occupied by a house and workshop, the rear by kitchens, other service rooms, garden, well, and cesspool. A stone vaulted cellar was sunk half into the ground and reached by a short flight of steps. Here goods were manufactured, displayed, and sold—as they continue to be in Middle Eastern countries. Another short flight rose up to the house which might well have two-storey ends to a single storey hall in the medieval rural manner but roofed with a gable facing the street. Most town houses were timber framed above the cellar. Temporary booths between the two flights of steps were often roofed and incorporated in the main building to produce an upper gallery as in the 'Rows' of Chester.

b. During the latter part of the Middle Ages, the half-subterranean cellar appears to have passed out of favour. Instead, storage cellars were sometimes provided below ground and the shop rose to ground floor level where it occupied the front portion of a house. As the shop might be separately let, there was often no intercommunication with the house. At this time pressure on the most valuable land was leading to multi-storey development, especially making use of jettied construction, and development within the gardens was beginning.

c. wide frontage house with passage across hall giving access to rear of site.

d. narrow frontage house with passage alongside front rooms giving access to the courtyards and further buildings within the site.

Urban Vernacular: 16th and 17th Centuries

During this period medieval urban house plans were transformed through greater attention to heating, to privacy, and to access from floor to floor as houses grew ever taller.

Open hearths and charcoal braziers were replaced by fireplaces, flues and chimney stacks, reducing danger from fire and asphyxiation and increasing the number of rooms which could be heated. Both back-to-back fireplaces and those on party walls were used; the former gave a compact plan, retained heat within the house and gave a good distribution of warmth within narrow rooms; the latter simplified planning but sometimes gave problems in the design of party walls and took valuable space within the width of narrow sites. The open hall was finally abandoned and the practice of opening one room off another fell out of use, rooms being reached from corridors or internal lobbies. At the same time pressure on space within valuable sites encouraged development on several storeys on as much of the site as could be daylit. The winding staircase remained in use but placed centrally within the building and with fairly generous dimensions; such a staircase could be placed neatly against the jambs of back-to-back fireplaces but easier newel and dogleg staircases were also used, and the position at the rear of the building finally became most popular.

Towards the end of the 17C. the universal terrace house plan was developed. Having a lobby and staircase against the two rooms on each floor it could be used singly, in pairs or be repeated in terraced rows. This plan remained popular throughout the 18C. and 19C.

At the beginning of the 16C. most urban houses were timber framed and many had thatched roofs; at the end of the 17C. nearly all newly-built town houses were of brick or stone walls with a slate or tiled roof. Such materials were both fashionable and fire-resistant and many of the older houses were modernized and given fire-protection through the use of them: timber panelled gables towards the street were replaced by hipped roofs half-hidden behind a brick parapet, though often the timber framed party walls remained and, visible along the passages which led to the rear of each site, served as a reminder of the more ancient buildings underneath.

a. narrow frontage house with back-to-back fire-places and staircase against the fireplace jambs; corridor giving access to the rear of the site.

b. narrow frontage house with party wall fireplaces, central staircase and longitudinal passage.

c. wide frontage house with back-to-back fireplaces and rear staircase projection.

d. narrow frontage terrace house plan of late 17C. with one party wall fire-place and one corner fireplace; projecting closet at rear; no means of access through house to remainder of site.

Urban Vernacular:
18th and 19th Centuries

These notes outline developments in urban vernacular architecture between the close of the medieval period, towards the end of the 16C. and the beginning of the transformation of towns in the 19C. During this period market towns benefited from the general increase in population and agricultural productivity and, especially towards the end of the 18C., from improvements in transport. The coming of the railways from 1830 onwards meant rapid development of those served by the main lines but slow decay of the towns by-passed. The rise of factory based industry meant the establishment of some new towns and the transformation of many villages and some small market towns into tightly built settlements.

During the early part of the period, urban vernacular was characterized by the development of long thin buildings or rows of houses along the length of narrow medieval plots. A passage through the completely built-up front of the plot led to a footpath or alleyway; facing on to the footpath, and so at right angles to the street, new buildings occupied the former outbuildings and garden of the medieval house.

But during the later years of the period the most characteristic urban vernacular was in the development of terraces and squares, and in the grounds of the large houses which had been built as the town houses of country landowners. The most spectacular examples of such development in, e.g., London, Edinburgh, and Bath, were architect-designed and out of the vernacular field, but few towns are without the provincial craftsman's version of these fashionable terraces. Some of the new towns of the early Industrial Revolution (e.g. Whitehaven) are built entirely in this manner.

At the same time, there was a great deal of reconstruction and refacing on the original sites in medieval towns to produce a narrow, tall, single fronted building—house or shop—or a similar façade on an earlier plan.

170

The typical town house of the 18C. combined the arrangement of rooms on several levels connected by a staircase with the newly fashionable horizontal grouping of individual houses to produce a unified elevation. Service rooms, even in vernacular buildings, might be confined to the basement, sometimes the principal rooms were at first floor level, but usually the ground floor provided living-rooms, the first floor bedrooms, and the second floor or garret space was available for the bedrooms of children and servants. At this time most new houses in towns were built of brick with tiles or slated roofs, though other materials continued in use.

a. alternative with central staircase.

Minor Industrial Vernacular:
Early Cottage Industry

For as long as domestic manufacture continued at subsistence level throughout the country, we could not expect to see any reflection of manufacture in the form of the dwelling house. But as machinery was gradually introduced and improved, as manufacturing operations became more specialized, and as changes in industrial organization led to larger scale operations, so these developments came to be reflected to a greater and greater extent in buildings. In some parts of the country, domestic manufacture never developed beyond the subsistence level, but in others especially in the Southern Pennines and in the Eastern Midlands the manufacturing processes left the home and became concentrated in factories.

During the early part of this development two stages may be distinguished: modification of a living-room for the accommodation of simple machinery, and provision of a separate room as a work place. Both developments could occur as modification or extension of an existing house, or could form the basis of new construction.

In the textile industries at least, these early industrial adaptations were more likely to occur in rural rather than urban situations. As the hand loom weavers of Oldham found to their cost, a life dependent on one trade was too uncertain, and those with the luxury of choice preferred to be able to switch between manufacture and agriculture according to the season and the state of trade. In rural locations these early industrial cottages might be built singly or in pairs, but in both country and towns cottages were also built in blocks of four or in terraces.

Construction was of brick or stone, according to locality, though modification of earlier timber framed houses may sometimes be seen.

In this example, apparently of the late 16C., an extension of the main living-room provided space which was near the heat and winter light of the fire on the hearth, but was out of the way of domestic activities. This space was lit by a long window of ten lights divided by diamond mullions, which was quite the largest window of the house. It seems more than likely that the extension represents an early adaptation of a house for cottage industry.

In the examples illustrated, based on early 19C. cottages at Hathern, Leicestershire, the front ground floor room and the two first floor rooms provided domestic accommodation while the rear ground floor room accommodated stocking frames and was lit by a large, four-light window. The position of the staircase, rising from the living-room, meant that the work-room could be separately let without loss of privacy in the cottage.

173

Minor Industrial Vernacular:
Later Cottage Industry

Such was the erratic progress of invention in the textile industry during the late 18C. and early 19C. that increased capacity in one part of the trade entailed shortage of capacity and therefore industrial prosperity in some other part. As an example of this situation, factory based and water powered cotton spinning placed such demands on the hand loom weavers that their prosperity was unprecedented, and they could afford to invest in specialized buildings for their craft, though still operating on a domestic basis.

Even when production of the coarser textiles had become concentrated in factories, the finer qualities, and work in more expensive materials and processes, continued on hand-powered machinery operated by craftsmen at home.

For the industrial parts of the house most textile trades at least had the following requirements:—

good daylight—e.g. from windows extending as far along the wall as structural stability would allow; *controlled ventilation*—e.g. where a smoke and dust free atmosphere was essential, and only a few small lights were made openable; *unobstructed space*—e.g. a space unobstructed by walls or piers most easily obtained under the roof; *provision for storage*—e.g. a loft in the attic space above the machinery; *access for goods and workers*—in some trades a hoist and 'taking-in hole' was necessary for raw material. As the work room might be let separately from the house, and as non-resident labour might be employed, access was arranged to intrude as little as possible on the privacy of the house; *heating*—e.g. a fireplace or brazier, but varied with the trade.

In the residential parts of the house, the artisan would have a kitchen and scullery on the ground floor and two bedrooms above; but, some-

174

times, one of a small group of such industrial houses would have larger and slightly more pretentious accommodation.

These buildings were erected both in the country and in the expanding towns, sometimes in groups of two or four, but more commonly in short terraces. They continued to be built until about the middle of the 19C., long after the factory-based textile industry had become established, but some of the later examples were so designed that they could alternate between purely domestic and partly industrial use according to the state of trade.

A master hosier's house from Winston Magna, Leicestershire, consists of a two-storey building with fairly conventional domestic accommodation, but attached to it there is a two-storey workshop, both floors being well-lit by very long mullioned windows, the upper being approached by ladder and trapdoor from the lower, and both provided with fireplaces.

The old-established silk-manufacturing town of Macclesfield in Cheshire includes scores of examples of buildings designed for cottage industry as well as several elegant factories. In the terrace illustrated, the cutaway diagram shows the conventional 'two up and two down' of the domestic accommodation and the well-lit unobstructed floor space of the weaving loft. The rear staircase provided access to the loft in a relatively discreet manner and sometimes party walls were modified to allow several lofts to run together.

Urban Industrial Houses: Earlier

We have seen that from the latter half of the 18C. onwards it became normal for even the poorest families to be housed in dwellings built of materials permanent enough to survive to the present day. During this period, cottages were built by land-owners for the labourers on their tenants' farms, by the owners of mines and quarries which were located so far away from existing settlements that new construction was unavoidable, by mill-owners when, in the days of water-power, sites on streams in remote valleys were customary for factories, and by private landlords for the workers in the towns. Throughout the period it was customary for lodgers to be boarded by working class families, and many of the complaints of overcrowding sprang from this practice, which was, of course, largely unavoidable during this period of swift industrialization. At the same time, the ancient process of 'filtering down' continued, whereby large houses built for wealthier families were later divided and occupied by the poor. But also, both in town and country, a certain amount of philanthropic provision of 'model' or 'improved' dwellings for the poor helped to ensure an eventual and general improvement.

Throughout the period the plan and sectional form, and the material and construction of cottages, did not differ substantially between rural developments, urbanized miners' villages, and entirely urban situations. The difference was more a matter of location and degree, the 'two up and two down' appearing quite different in a terrace of three in a pretty village than in a long roadside terrace on a bleak moor.

Regional variations in plan form and materials emphasize the vernacular qualities of these cottages. For instance, miners and quarrymen tended to have single-storey dwellings, hence the long low terraces of the Pennines, of Northumberland, and of Devon, and the 'Croglofft' cottages of Caernarvonshire; while textile workers tended to have two-storey houses, the residue of design for cottage industry. The steep sided valleys of the Lancashire and Yorkshire Pennines led to the development of the extraordinary 'houses-on-top-of-houses'; Leeds and Sheffield preferred the back-to-back. And yet the non-industrialized communities of East Anglia and South Eastern England continued to build cottages in timber and clay, closely following their own traditions.

The individual cottage was a perfectly adequate setting for contemporary family life, but when multiplied beyond count and unsupported by the services which community life required, it was inadequate and developed the bad reputation which it now endures.

a

b

Part of the surrealist quality of a mining village, all the more extreme now that so many have been abandoned, comes from the use of long terraces or courtyards of tightly packed cottages to give a curiously urban character to an isolated rural community (*b*). Often the effect is heightened by the use of single-storey cottages each consisting of two rooms, a living-room and a partitioned bedroom, in reincarnation of a medieval plan (*a*).

c

The two-storey workers' cottage which preceded the Public Health Act of 1875 usually consisted of a living kitchen and scullery/wash-house on the ground floor and two bedrooms above. Access was by a door opening directly off the street, with the living kitchen screened only by a timber 'speer'. At the rear a short yard, sometimes individual, sometimes communal, contained earth closet and coal store (*c*).

177

Urban Industrial Houses: Later

Various lines of development converged to ensure that the terraced row of cottages became the urban domestic vernacular of the second half of the 19C. But while the form of the individual dwelling had been crystallized the form of the terraced layout took longer to establish and depended at least partly in developments in sanitation.

As long as cottages were erected in twos and threes in scattered villages no serious sanitary problems arose and if rooms were tiny, space around buildings was plentiful, while fresh air was plentiful and unpolluted. Even when terraces of cottages were built to serve isolated mines or mills the sanitary problems, though more severe, were still at the village scale and capable of solution by traditional methods.

In the rapidly expanding towns, however, the scale was unprecedented and new solutions were necessary. In the older parts of towns, the ground available in long medieval plots for sanitation and water supplies diminished until cesspool and well occupied adjacent holes. In the newer parts, terraces and courts were built by developers who had neither powers nor incentive to ensure adequate water supply and sanitary arrangements. Disease and epidemic were the inevitable result and the reports of the 19C. Committees of Inquiry are full of detailed accounts of revolting conditions around the dwellings and overcrowding within.

The method of sanitation eventually adopted was based on the regular removal of night soil, neutralized by earth or ashes, from individual privies located at the rear, at an appropriate distance from each dwelling. Convenience and economy suggested the back ally and a grid-iron street layout, and it was not until waterborne sewage systems brought the WC within the house that the back street, for sanitary purposes, could be eliminated and alternative layouts adopted.

Thus the design of the cottage had developed, typologically, from two rooms and a loft on a piece of the village common to the four rooms and two full storeys of high density urban development. The reaction which followed began with a return to an idealized village of one and a half storey cottages.

The true back-to-back houses had only one wall exposed to light and air, and, from their absence of through ventilation have gained a reputation as the most unhealthy of the 19C. slums. Once again it is the repetition and concentration of quite a normal vernacular domestic plan which was really at fault. In the most extreme examples, houses facing on to the streets were backed by other houses facing each other over a narrow courtyard containing the earth closets and reached by way of narrow passages through the buildings.

The Public Health Act of 1875 having required local authorities to make bye-laws to govern standards of construction and space about dwellings and having established effective enforcement machinery, a uniform pattern of housing began to spread over the country and to supersede local variations. In the houses illustrated, based on examples dated 1883, the traditional two-storey cottage plan was maintained but with tall rooms and large windows providing ventilation and short front gardens and long backyards providing the required space about dwellings. Back streets or alleys enabled the improved sanitation of the period to be adopted.

179

Minor Industrial Vernacular: Windmills and Watermills

Until the coming of the steam engine, power was available from wind, water, or muscle. The use of each power source has left its mark in the form of vernacular buildings.

The use of the muscular power of the horse to drive farm machinery has already been described and illustrated. Similar motive power was used for industrial purposes in mines and a few early factories, and indeed the horse engine known to have been employed in the coalfields of Northumberland, Durham and West Cumberland in the early 18C., may have provided the inspiration for the horse powered versions of the first threshing machines when employed in those districts. But virtually nothing remains of buildings to house industrial horse engines.

Wind and water driven mills have a long history and many examples still survive. Their use was largely though not entirely complementary, windmills serving the low-lying corn growing countryside of East Anglia, the Fylde, etc. where rivers are wide and sluggish, watermills serving the rest of the country where a regular and reliable flow of water was combined with a useful head. There were also a few mills operated by tides. Windmills were chiefly used for grinding corn or pumping water, watermills were used for these purposes and for an increasing range of industrial processes from fulling cloth to slitting iron.

The design of the actual machinery driven by wind and water power is far beyond the scope of vernacular architecture and its study has been carefully undertaken and well reported, but the buildings containing this machinery exercised the design and constructional ability of the vernacular craftsmen and a note is included here as a reminder of the range of design ability and constructional skills needed by these untutored members of the rural community.

180

Most windmills were either post mills (a) or tower mills (b). In the former, the whole chamber containing gears and millstones could be rotated according to the direction of the wind and therefore a light, usually weather boarded, timber framed structure was carried on an open timber base or a squat brick tapered cylinder. In the latter only the cap could be turned and the machinery was contained within a brick or weather boarded tower. The cutaway isometric shows a typical smock mill (c).

The usual arrangement in a watermill was to enclose the milling machinery and other ancillary accommodation in a weather boarded, brick, or stone building alongside the mill race which turned the one or two wheels which projected from the building. Except when undershot wheels were used this meant that the building had to master the slope between headrace and tailrace. (d) Cutaway view showing mill with attached corn-drying kiln; (e), (f), Diagrammatic section through kiln and mill.

Minor Industrial Vernacular:
Smithies, Kilns and Textile Mills

Among the most ubiquitous of vernacular industrial buildings are the smithies; among the most aesthetically pleasing are the kilns and furnaces; and among the most massive and structurally adventurous are the textile mills.

The smithy was usually a small rectangular building open to the roof and with space for storage, space for working and space for the hearth. At one end of the building was the hearth with its bellows and fuel store; at the other end were the racks for tools, items of equipment and part finished metal; in between was the working area, well-lit and ventilated from the open door and big enough for horse shoeing in wet weather. Outside was another working area including space for shrinking tyres on wooden wheels. Most surviving smithies are fairly late in date— mid to late 19C., built of brick or stone and virtually without ornament; many have been lost in later garages and light engineering works.

Kilns included those in which limestone was converted into lime, those in which pottery was baked, those used in glass-making and those used in firing bricks or tiles. Limekilns were usually built into a slope, often an outcrop of limestone itself, so that alternate layers of limestone and fuel could be fed from the top and lime drawn out from the aperture at the bottom. The great arch over this aperture was made out of crude but massive stone voussoirs and the hidden shape of the kiln chamber was often gracefully formed. Pottery kilns made of brick and bottle-shaped were once common in the Stoke area but most have been destroyed; however, many country potteries still remain with small kilns of the same type. Pottery kilns were hollow, almost invariably made of brick, and usually reinforced with iron bands to counteract the cracks inevitable when one hot dry surface on the interior married with the cold wet external surface. Glass kilns were somewhat similar in principle but cone-shaped and with a furnace for heating the molten glass in the middle. Brick and tile kilns were squat or cupola-shaped.

The iron furnaces of the 18C. consisted of a stone furnace tower fed with fuel and ore from storage sheds at an upper level, and attended by great water powered bellows at a lower level.

Water-powered textile mills made use of some of the devices and designs of watermills for corn grinding and developed designs and constructional methods used in later steam-powered factories. The corn mill was a compact building making use of several levels to take off the power as close as possible to the water-wheel itself; similarly the textile mill used several storeys just long enough to take power by way of a shaft from the wheel without too much loss in efficiency and just wide enough to take several machines in depth without losing too much daylight from the outer walls. Even with the light machinery of the period it was impossible to span from wall to wall, and slender cast-iron columns were devised to give intermediate support to the timber beams. Mills had windows of domestic proportions and domestic details which helped to give a dignity rarely found in other industrial buildings.

a. smithy plan.
b. general view of smithy.
c. pottery kiln.
d. glass cone.
e. lime kiln.
f. textile mill with domestic proportions, cast iron intermediate columns, roof truss giving space on top floor.

7. COMPARISONS AND CONCLUSION

Walling and Roofing Materials: an example of local distribution

The intricate pattern of the use of walling materials cannot yet be adequately demonstrated on a national scale, but sufficient work has been done in some districts for the local pattern to be shown. One such district, the Solway Plain, has been taken as an example. The position of the district is shown on the diagram and the scale is indicated by a grid of 10km. squares. The maps are based on records made in the field of some 1,200 examples of domestic vernacular architecture built before about 1840.

The maps of walling material show how the basic geological formation of the district has determined the broad division between limestone, sandstone and clay, how the area of early use of clay roughly corresponds with that of the later use of brick, and how the use of the superior sandstone encroaches on those parts where the inferior limestone was the indigenous material.

The maps of roofing material show that thatching remained in use in districts which were distant from the quarries of the superior sandstone flags or Lake District slates. Nevertheless flags were used for superior buildings in all the lowland areas while Lake District slates came into universal use in the district once improved transport made them available.

184

Lowland and Highland Building Regions

The diagrammatic map (after P. Smith) shows a rich inner lowland region, a rather less rich outer lowland region, an intermediate region sharing highland and lowland characteristics, and an English and Welsh highland zone. Scotland and Ireland have further outer highland characteristics. Early farm-houses are rare in the highland zone; early farm-houses are plentiful in the inner lowland zone.

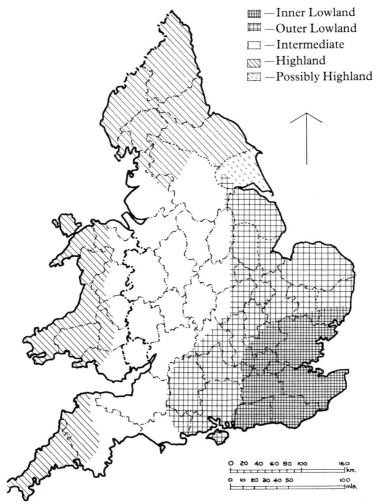

— Inner Lowland
— Outer Lowland
— Intermediate
— Highland
— Possibly Highland

Walling and Roofing Materials: examples of national distribution

Although no adequate national survey of vernacular architecture has yet been completed it is possible to illustrate in broad terms the pattern of use of certain walling and roofing materials, certain structural systems and certain plan types. The following very generalised maps are based on two sets of dot maps: one consisting of some 500 examples taken mainly from published sources and not evenly spread through the country and the other consisting of some 1200 examples evenly spread and taken partly from records of the Manchester University School of Architecture, partly from records of the Royal Commissions on Historical Monuments and partly from published sources. The map of cruck construction is based on those in Dr. N. Alcock's *Catalogue of Cruck Buildings*. The tentative distributions of plan types depend on information which is not evenly available over the country; they depend partly on external observation and do not take into account the date or social level at which the plan-type was used.

Time Scales

An attempt (p. 199) has been made to show some time scales for window and door shape and mouldings. They are based on information from the North West of England, the West Midlands, Monmouthshire and part of Oxfordshire only. Not all the information is available in a compatible form. Distinction between use of the various details at Large House, Small House, and Cottage levels has been illustrated. Time scales for roofing materials have been prepared from the same information and shown in the same manner.

Walling Materials: stone

hard rocks and slates
sandstones
carboniferous limestone
gritstones
coal measure sandstones
lias limestone
magnesium limestone
oolitic limestone
greensand

0 20 40 60 80 100   160
0 10 20 30 40 50   100

stone walling—shows the Pennine and Welsh mountain districts, the moor-lands of South West England, the limestone belt, and the Weald, but there are many other smaller patches of use. The building stones are indicated in a very general way, they combine some stones which appear similar but are geologically different, and they take no account of the intricate local variations found in many parts of the country.

Walling Materials: flint, pebble and cobble

FLINT
PEBBLE
COBBLE

0 20 40 60 80 100   160 km.
0 10 20 30 40 50   100 mls.

flint, pebble and cobble—the flint belt of the east and south-east is shown; pebble and cobble walling is found in many small patches of which only some of the most important can be shown.

Walling Materials: brick

BRICK

O 20 40 60 80 100 160 km.
O 10 20 30 40 50 100 mls.

brick—generally the areas of brick walling complement those of stone; brick usually replaced timber frame.

Walling Materials: clay, etc.

CLAY ETC

clay, etc.—the map shows the districts in which substantial numbers survive and distinguishes the clay lump technique of East Anglia.

Timber Frame: cruck construction

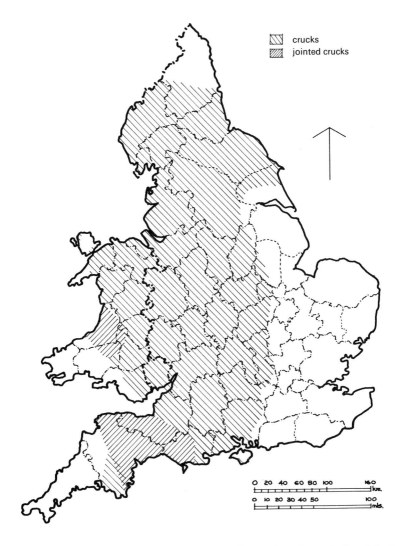

cruck construction—areas where jointed crucks are found are distinguished from those with true crucks.

Timber Walling

exposed timber frame (half timbering)—the map shows areas in which half timbering is commonly found and distinguishes between areas in which narrow panels predominate (vertical hatching) and areas in which square panels predominate (cross hatching).

Timber Walling: cladding materials

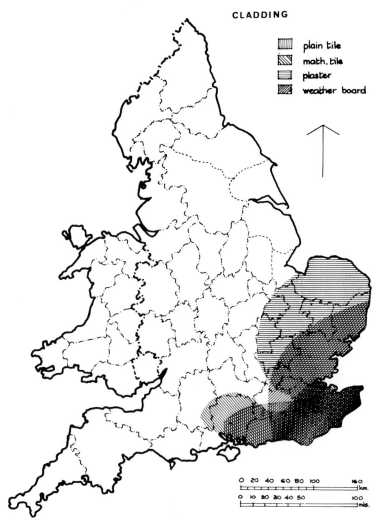

CLADDING

⦀	plain tile
▨	math. tile
☰	plaster
▧	weather board

cladding materials to timber frame are virtually confined to the east and south east, districts vary somewhat, though all materials are found in East Kent.

Roofing Materials: thatch

THATCH

thatch roofing—though varying in density, most parts of the country retain some thatched buildings.

Roofing Materials: stone flags and stone tiles

STONE FLAGS
TILES

0 20 40 60 80 100   160 km.
0 10 20 30 40 50   100 mls.

stone flag and tile roofing—the map distinguishes between the stone flags of the Pennines and the stone tiles of the Cotswolds, Wales, and the Weald.

Roofing Materials: plain tiles and pantiles

PLAIN TILES
PANTILES

O 20 40 60 80 100 160 km.
O 10 20 30 40 50 100 mls.

pantiles and plain tiles—the former are generally confined to the east and north-east, the latter to the south-east, south, and Midlands of England.

Fireplaces

passage behind fireplace

front side-wall fireplace

O 20 40 60 80 100   160 km.

O 10 20 30 40 50   100 mls.

two-unit and cross-passage houses—areas of common use are shown.
fireplace in front side wall—areas in South-West Wales and South-West England where these may be seen are shown; no attempt has been made to indicate halls with side wall fireplaces at the rear.

Fireplaces (continued)

central fireplaces plan (lobby entrance)—areas where these houses may be found are indicated.

Time Scales: windows, doors, roofing

WINDOW SHAPE

	1500	1550	1600	1650	1700	1750	1800	1850	
gothic									L.S.c.
mullioned									L.S.c.
square									L.S.c.
tall									L.S.c

MOULDINGS

cavetto									L.S.c
splay									L.S.c.
square cut									L.S.c.
architrave									L.S.c.

DOORWAY SHAPE

pointed arch									L.S.c
sub-medieval									L.S.c.
early ren.									L.S.c.
later ren.									L.S.c

ROOFING MATERIALS

	1500	1550	1600	1650	1700	1750	1800	1850	
thatch				? ?					L.S.c.
stone flags									L.S.c
tiles									L.S.c
slate									L.S.c.

Vernacular Architecture in North America: A Note on English Influence

The next few pages include a few comments on the vernacular architecture of North America considered as a regional variation of English vernacular.

English influence on American vernacular was never without challenge. During the colonial period, the English colonists shared the settled territory with Dutch, Swedes, and Spaniards on the Eastern Seaboard, with the Spanish and French in the Gulf of Mexico, and with the French over most of Canada; the colonists of each nationality looked to their own homeland for architectural inspiration and their craftsmen brought over the traditional skills of each separate country. After the Revolution, the influence of supporting European nations, especially France, was naturally preferred to that of England and it is generally assumed that the greater significance of the Greek Revival in American domestic vernacular has some political basis. The great period of expansion in the later 19C. reinforced the influence of Central Europe which had begun to show itself in Pennsylvania during the early 18C. Nevertheless, the English has probably been the greatest single contribution to American vernacular.

Since there are several notable scholars working in the field, the current wave of interest in vernacular architecture has now gained the impetus in the United States which it has in this country. Domestic vernacular is still partly a study of individual monuments; in spite of the image only recently lost of America as a nation of farmers, very little appears to have been published on farm buildings; while, again, with a few important exceptions, systematic study of early industrial buildings has been neglected. On the other hand the preservation of material in the form of buildings in situ or moved together as open-air museums is very extensive and strikes a nostalgic chord in the mind of the American tourist.

For the English student of vernacular architecture, North America can provide valuable comparative material. In the first place it can show, for a short period at least, another English region, one which was culturally English, climatically not radically different but was subject to special local influences. This other English region is comparatively well documented—the measured drawings of the Historic American Buildings Survey are usually convincing and comprehensive, and genealogical self-interest as well as historical sense has provided documentary history for individual vernacular buildings not commonly available on this side of the Atlantic.

Secondly, it can show parallel and divergent development of planning and construction from common origins. The house plans recently classified in Cambridgeshire were employed in New England and developed simultaneously for a period, the corresponding constructional forms had a similar development except that in East and South-East England lightweight framing was developed for domestic use in a very small area even though widely adopted for industrial and transport buildings, while in America, lightweight framing became universal and is still the normal method of constructing all low buildings.

Thirdly the larger country and greater population has led to preservation of vernacular practices through geographical isolation or deliberate cultural isolation. Thus the student of English vernacular architecture ought to be able to profit just as much as the student of English vernacular speech from the inbred communities of the Appalachians; and the strict puritan sects of Pennsylvania preserve to the present day the communal erection process and appropriate constructional forms which were once normal here on this side of the Atlantic.

However, it would be quite wrong to give comparative American material disproportionate weight. The great vernacular tradition of the hewn log construction in America appears to owe nothing to English influence though it may speak volumes for British adaptability. It is only claimed that for a hundred years or so after the middle of the 17C. there was yet another Great Rebuilding of England, but this time on the other side of the Atlantic.

Vernacular Architecture in North America: English Influence on the Northern half of the Colonies

The groups who formed most of the original English colonies north of the Dutch settlements on the Hudson River were deliberately attempting to create a society which was not a copy of the stratified society they had left. Their homes, therefore, tended to be more uniform in size than in the districts they had left, Large Houses and Cottages being few, Small Houses, appropriate to yeoman status being the normal.

As the names of many of their settlements suggest, East Anglia and the South East provided the early immigrants. They brought over the plan types to which they had been accustomed; one room deep, two storeys in height, central chimneys placed back to back, and the corresponding structural forms, box-frame of heavy timber sections, light studded wall and independent roof construction. The surviving buildings show that the early wattle and daub panels proved inadequate for severe winters and were quickly replaced by weather boards (or clapboards). To the two fireplaces of the original plan two further fireplaces for first floor chambers were added, and often a heated extension or 'ell' was added at the rear.

During the period in question (late 17C. and early 18C.) plans with a continuous outshut at the rear, roofed by an extension from the main roof were often found on the English side of the Atlantic as well as the American, where they were called 'saltbox'. The double pitch, or gambrel roof was also used in common. Again the widespread use of masonry details imitated in painted timber on the fronts of timber framed houses recalls similar practices in South-Eastern England.

a. The illustration shows an example of a 17C. house in New England. The Ironmasters House, at Saugus, Massachussetts, was built about 1640 as part of the development of a water powered ironworks on the site. The house has been altered and restored at various times but survives as a good example of the American equivalent of contemporary work in Eastern and South Eastern England.

b. and *c*. Ground floor and first plans of the Ironmasters House.

d. cross-section through 'saltbox' house with main roof extending down to cover rear outshut.

e. isometric of saltbox house.

f., *g*., and *h*. Details of upper floor construction (after Kelly). *f*. true jettied first floor, with pendants, *g*. false jettying, *h*. hewn post without jettying.

i. and *j*. sketch and plan of single-cell house.

k. sketch showing commonly used gambrel roof.

Vernacular Architecture in North America: English Influence in the Southern Colonies

The earliest permanent English settlement on the Atlantic coast was made in 1607 at Jamestown, Virginia. Intensive excavation of the long-abandoned site of the colony, together with the many surviving examples of 17C. and 18C. domestic architecture in the South have combined to build a picture of a vernacular different from that of New England. This difference reflected a different social organization. Most of the Southern colonies were plantations made by individual proprietors or companies of investors as commercial enterprises and reflected all the grades of wealth and social status to be found in England. But beneath this social ladder was another formed of the slaves who were a vital part of the special agricultural and domestic economy. Thus, examples of domestic architecture range from the pretentious Palladian compositions of e.g. Westover, Charles City County, Virginia, to the flimsy slaves' quarters of which only fragments remain. Only a proportion fall within the vernacular range. Of these many preserve a plan one room in depth but with gable chimneys, and some retain the projecting porch and staircase common throughout England at the turn of the 17C. Although most homes were timber-framed, a good proportion of the surviving examples are of brick with similar elaboration of chimney stack and gable wall to contemporary work in Eastern and South Eastern England.

Further developments reflected the more temperate climate of this part of the Continent. In the summer and on the coastal plain breezes were to be attracted and shade sought, therefore the plans developed in forms extended and protected by verandahs rather than as compact blocks and with multiple fireplaces as further north.

a. Bacon's Castle,
   Surrey County,
   Virginia, said to
   have been built 1655,
   brick walls, elaborate
   gables and chimney
   stacks, projecting
   multi-storey porches.
b. Typical 17C. house
   plans.
c. houses extended by
   verandahs.
d. single-cell timber
   frame house, pro-
   jecting brick chimney.
e. two-cell 'Virginia
   House'.
f. as *e.* but with rooms
   in roof space.
g. two-cell, two-storey
   house with attached
   kitchen at rear and
   two-storey, 'porch'
   or verandah at the
   front.
h. brick house of
   double-pile plan.

Vernacular Architecture in Scotland

The vernacular architecture of Scotland developed differently from that of England and recent advances in its study suggest that some note should be included here by way of comparison.

Outside the towns, rural settlement over much of Scotland was based on *fermtouns*, townships of half a dozen families who tilled their land in common according to the 'run-rig' system of intensive cultivation of a well-manured infield and occasional cultivation of part of the rough pasture outfield. In the *fermtouns* the landlord–tenant relationship as well as the poverty of the people perpetuated the use of primitive structures of short life. From about 1750 to 1880, however, there was a great wave of 'improvement' whereby the *fermtouns* were replaced by individual farmsteads serving large farms of land enclosed in fields and including farm-houses, farm buildings and labourers' cottages. All the new structures were substantially built and provided living conditions much better than those they had replaced. Some farmsteads were designed by professional architects or agriculturalists and were in the forefront of farmstead design but others perpetuated the plans of earlier buildings. In parts of the Highlands and Islands, nevertheless, the traditional plans and methods of construction persisted until quite late in the 19C.

Within the bigger towns, medieval systems of land-holding perpetuated the use of tall multi-storey buildings, often retaining timber frame

206

at least on the street frontage. The smaller towns took part in the architecture of the agricultural revolution and over 100 new planned villages and towns were founded and built.

Although the buildings of Scotland now appear as solidly built of dressed stone, such substantial construction was confined to a relatively small number of important buildings such as churches and defensible dwellings until about 200 years ago. Most houses and farm buildings were built of clay, wattle, or various combinations of field stones and turf. Solid clay-walled structures, comparable with those of Cumberland survive here and there, especially in South West Scotland. Clay and timber were used as 'stake and rice' in walls comparable with the mud and stud of Lincolnshire. 'Clay and bool' walls alternated stones or cobbles with clay and turf. Brick walls were used in the Central Lowlands and parts of the North East from the late 18C. but sometimes as an inner lining to a wall of some other material. Thick walls of outer and inner skins of rough stone with an interior of two or three feet of turf were characteristic of the 'blackhouses' of North and West Scotland. Conventional masonry walls of the late 18C. and 19C. included the techniques of pointing in lime mortar and harling, a roughcast with dry dash which concealed the stones behind a whitish surface.

Cruck construction was once widespread in Scotland though surviving examples are few and usually of rough and spindly timber. Jointed crucks were common and the upright parts often survive in ruined buildings which have lost their roofs. End crucks were used to produce the rounded hipped-roof shape. For although most of the buildings of the Scottish countryside now present gabled slated roofs to the observer, the use of hipped roofs of thatch was normal before the late 18C. There were many regional variations but thatch of wheat or rye straw over a turf underthatch was commonly used. In the South West and North East heather was often used in place of straw. Broom or whin was a cheaper substitute while divots or squares of turf laid diamond fashion were used to cover inferior buildings. In the Northern Isles, especially, the thatch was kept in position with weighted nets of rope. Everywhere thatch was a material which required constant attention and frequent replacement. From the early 19C. on, slate quarried locally or imported from the Lake District or Snowdonia and carried on roofs of sawn softwood superseded the thatch. Flagstones of sandstone were an alternative available here and there. Felt roofs of cloth dipped in tar were a later Scottish development.

The well-known 'blackhouse' of remote Scotland consisted basically of a single rectangular room reached through a single door and accommodating humans and animals under the same roof. The houses and cottages of the improvement period usually had two habitable rooms on the ground floor, one or both containing box beds. From the mid to late 19C. rooms in the roof space were brought into use as bedrooms and lit by roof lights or dormer windows. Heating developed from the use of an open hearth set against a low fireback wall under a suspended chimney hood, via the 'hanging lum' of a hood cantilevered from a gable or transverse wall, to the use of a conventional fireplace, flue and chimney stack, nearly always set in a gable wall.

a. Clay-walled, thatched roof single-storey house as found in Dumfries-shire.
b. One-and-a-half storey house, widespread but here from Aberdeen-shire.
c. Horse-engine house, type widespread in the Lowlands.
d. Two-storey house with pantile roof as found in Fife.
e. Aberdeen Bond of large blocks of stone separated by small stones.
f. One-and-a-half storey house with dormers and roof light, widespread but here from the Borders.
g. House with rough boulder walls and corrugated galvanized roof replacing thatch; as to be seen in the Western Isles.
h. Upper-storey town house as found in Fife and Perthshire.
i. Blackhouse as re-erected at Kingussie in the Grampians.
j. Tower-house.

a

b

c

d

e

f

g

h

i

j

209

Conclusion: The Vernacular Revival

We have seen that the closing years of the 19C. marked the end of any substantial vernacular content in even the humblest dwelling houses, farm buildings, or minor industrial buildings in this country. By 1900, the rich, middle classes, and poor alike could afford substantial dwelling houses in permanent materials; their houses were subject to building regulations national in origin even if local in administration; the choice of materials and constructional methods was wider than ever, but walls of mass-produced bricks and roofs of easily quarried slate were so cheap and universally available that any other choice was almost wilful; while large architectural practices operating nationally, their innovations immediately published in magazines of wide circulation, left little demand for regional variation.

And yet if one were to count separately many of the architectural details mentioned in this book, they could be shown to have been used more frequently in the 50 years after 1900 than the centuries before that date. The housing estates of the 1930s display more half-timbered gables than will ever be recorded in Worcestershire or Kent for they represent the ill-digested, speculative builder's version of the Vernacular Revival style which was dominant in English—and indeed in American—domestic architecture from about 1860 to 1914.

Minor domestic architecture had previously given inspiration to sophisticated designers as part of the Picturesque Movement of the late 18C. and early 19C. Details only just passing out of use—such as decora-

210

tively thatched roofs—were adopted by the fashionable designers and multiplied and magnified to produce vast 'cottages' for their clients. When picturesque qualities provided the criteria and the demands of a selected external appearance were paramount, then details from many periods and locations could legitimately be combined in the same building. But the Vernacular Revival of the later 19C. was quite differently based. In 1861, J. L. Petit, becoming disillusioned with a Gothic Revival which conformed to medieval types rather than developed medieval principles, suggested that the basis of a living architecture was 'our ordinary or vernacular architecture'. He thus gave to minor domestic architecture something of the rank formerly restricted to churches, temples, palaces and tombs and related architecture to the everyday world of speech and the vulgar tongue at that, rather than the esoteric worlds of sculpture, painting or poetry. At the same time, William Morris and his colleagues in the Arts and Crafts Movement had been looking back to what they believed had been an age of simple unaffected craftsmanship. Honesty in materials and techniques was held to apply equally to architecture as to the related crafts of furniture making, fabric weaving, glass painting, etc. The result was a style of architecture in which some practitioners at least felt they were returning to the down-to-earth, vernacular spirit of the Middle Ages.

The principal architects working in the Vernacular Revival were Philip Webb, W. R. Lethaby, C. F. A. Voysey, M. H. Baillie Scott, Edgar Wood, and, from time to time, R. Norman Shaw and Sir Edwin Lutyens. Their opportunities came in the design of those medium sized country houses demanded by the members of the middle class who had been made rich enough by the Industrial Revolution to afford country retreats in the newly accessible Downs or Lake District. Their characteristic designs were for long, low, sprawling houses set beneath wide spreading roofs, broken with gables, emphasized by deep eaves, with long bands of mullioned windows, plain rendered wall surfaces, spidery wrought iron brackets, diamond paned lattices, and so on. An appearance of age and history was built into the houses by the incorporation, presumably deliberate, of details from several periods in the same building, and premature repair work in, e.g., the use of sloping buttresses on exposed corners. Many architects in the school, and especially E. S. Prior with his Norfolk flint houses, made conscious use of local materials. Some, Edgar Wood for instance, filled their sketchbooks with details of local cottages and farmhouses; and in some parts of the country the literature of vernacular architecture still relies on the published notes and drawings of such architects.

And so the Vernacular Revival, to judge from its completed monuments, appears to have taken its place in the ranks of architectural revivals of the 18C. and 19C., though further research will no doubt show to what extent it was differently based from the Greek, Gothic, and Italianate Revivals. Sensitive architects had felt the need for a style appropriate to the domestic circumstances of their clients, had seen the ingredients for such a style in the manor houses and farm-houses of various periods up and down the country, and combined these ingredients each one according to his own recipe, and, in most cases, had served up the results without much account of where they were to be enjoyed. The results were, indeed, usually as charming as they were comfortable, but they could not, by any classification, be called vernacular architecture.

Indeed it is hard to visualize any circumstances, short of the nuclear holocaust, which can possibly revive vernacular architecture in the country. The simple, unaffected, method of building which we call vernacular has been employed and then discarded at all levels of the social scale. The results of its employment make up a large but swiftly diminishing part of our present environment, they must be studied now, by this generation, or never.

(Opposite)

The illustration is of the set of drawings prepared by Edgar Wood in 1894 for a house, 'Barcroft' to be built in Bolton Road, Marland, Rochdale. Edgar Wood was an enthusiastic student of the vernacular architecture of the countryside around Manchester and prepared many sets of measured drawings and sketch-books of details.

Rochdale lies on the boundary zone between the timber frame and brick vernacular of the Lancashire Plain and the millstone grit vernacular of the Pennines and authentic details of both techniques have been included, e.g., from the Lowlands, shallow brick arches, brick string course with dentils, diaper work in projecting brick headers, thin millstone grit transomes and mullions, and from the Uplands, stone flagged roof, door with false three-centred arched head and carved device on the lintel, raised lintel over centre of gable window.

However, neither plan nor section appear to embody any local vernacular precedent, the particular mixture of brick arched heads and stone lintels appears wilful, the boldly projecting bay window at the north-west corner is not a local detail.

The drawing shows the house as it would appear in its old age with ridge-line sinking and chimneys leaning. It was not built so, but the desire of the architect to make his building of its own time and yet timeless, appears to have dominated his thinking.

(from *British Architect* Vol. 14, 1894, p. 382)

How to study vernacular architecture

a) General

The full fascination of vernacular architecture can only be enjoyed by study of a selected area or subject; and such study is likely to be most rewarding if conducted in a systematic manner. In the field of vernacular architecture perhaps more than in some other fields of study there is a constant temptation to explore the by-ways of folklore, dialect, country crafts, humble genealogy, water-colour sketching, etc. etc. but the ruthless and single-minded student will find ample reward in concentration on the buildings, their setting and the related documents.

In this field, as elsewhere, the scope of any study must be defined at the outset. The actual geographical area selected should be severely restricted in size; even the smallest and most unlikely community is likely to reveal an iceberg of information beneath the visible tip of a few unpromising buildings. The building type selected must be carefully defined; normally one starts with houses, but farm buildings or minor industrial buildings have the advantage that no one's privacy is impaired and, once the mystified owners have given access, repeated visits to deal with uncertain points do not usually present any difficulty. The period of study should also be firmly defined. There will usually be no difficulty in fixing the earliest date, but the choice of terminal date may be more debatable; dates of 1840 for houses and 1880 for farm buildings have been found useful in the past, but at this distance in time a continuation to, say, 1914, in both cases has a good deal to recommend it.

A complete study will result from simultaneous operation at three levels; extensive recording in some systematic manner, covering all relevant examples but in a superficial way; intensive recording of examples selected from the extensive survey as being typical or, in some other way likely to repay closer investigation; and documentary study, illuminating the surviving buildings and giving information on their forgotten predecessors.

b) Extensive Recording

A systematic procedure for the extensive study of examples of minor domestic architecture has been in use in the School of Architecture of the University of Manchester for some 20 years. It was devised by Professor Cordingley to assist in the speedy collection of survey material in the field, and, by reducing the subjective element as far as possible, to assist in the comparison of material between different parts of the country. The system was only intended to collect basic architectural information as revealed on the exterior of buildings and depended on intensive and documentary investigation to complete the study. The system has been reasonably successful in use up to date in meeting its limited objectives but does require a certain amount of experience and technical knowledge for satisfactory use. For the present purposes a simplified version based on the same principles is presented.

PROCEDURE:

1. *Define the Survey Area.* A civil parish provides a convenient area, and in most parts of England, at least, will include a village and some isolated houses.

2. *Assemble Materials.* A 2½ in. Ordnance Survey map, a field notebook, ball-point pens, preferably with separate colours for separate sets of notes, pencil for diagrams, camera and black-and-white film, and, if possible, field-glasses for reading datestones. The ideal method of transport is the pedestrian but bicycle, motor scooter, and motor car, in that order, would usually be used.

3. *Decide on the Relevant Period of the Building.* Some houses will be entirely of one build, but many will show evidence of work of several periods; it is important to decide which is the significant period—not necessarily the oldest—and note variations separately.

4. *Decide on Size-Type.* Ignoring Great Houses, each house will be either a Large House, a Small House, or a Cottage according to the wealth and status of its original occupant. One should distinguish between, say, Large Houses which have been subdivided, and Cottages built originally for cottagers. One should also bear in mind that the considerable variations in wealth between regions of the country meant that quite a small building might be a Large House in a poor district.

5. *Identify the Building.* A street address, if available, (and many houses in villages have no permanent address), the parish and county should be noted. A six-figure map reference as explained on the Ordnance Survey map should be given; this will include the reference letters of the 100km. square (e.g. NY) and the reference of the 100 m. square in which the building is located (e.g. 325·501), the total reference being

e.g. NY—325·501; it is also convenient to have a serial number for the surveyor's own use.

6. *Note Down the Aspect.* i.e. in what direction the front door is facing e.g. S.E.; this may be obtained by compass or, accurately enough for the present purpose, from the Ordnance Survey map.

7. *Note down the principal walling material.* i.e. stone, flint, cobble etc., brick, clay etc., timber frame (half-timbered, or with plain tile, math. tile, slate, weatherboard, plaster, cladding).

8. *Note down any reliably dated feature.* Many stone-walled buildings bear an inscribed date either on a door lintel, in a plaque over the door, or alongside a chimney stack. Brick walled buildings might have a date scratched on a brick, in a diaper pattern, or on stone dressings. Timber framed buildings sometimes have dates carved on the main bressummer of a jettied projection; or modelled in a plaster cladding. Any building may have a date cast in a lead rainwater head or cistern. None of these dates necessarily relates to the original construction, but all relate to some period in the life of a building and, taken with other evidence are of obvious importance.

9. *Note down salient features according to the code.* From each line of the code sheets illustrated on pages 218–19 select the appropriate alternative.

10. *Add a photograph and diagrammatic sketches.* A photograph alone is an inadequate record of a building. No single photograph can show enough of the exterior of a building nor, in fickle circumstances of light can quality be reliable. Diagrammatic sketches, however crude, are always useful and, really, indispensible.

11. *Note down initials and date of survey.* For comparative purposes the date at which a record is made is significant—and during the present wave of destruction and alteration of country property important for historical record.

DEVELOPMENT:

Any surveyor can develop any part of the code to meet his own requirements. For instance if there were a special interest in brickwork then A2 could be developed to record eight different bonds, e.g. A2.1 for English Bond, A2.2 for English Cross Bond and so on. Further codes could be developed for pointing whatever the bond, e.g. A2.11 for English Bond with a struck joint.

A record card made from an 8 in. by 5 in. filing card.

A completed record card. The coded description shows the house to have brick walling (A2), with a mixture of other materials (B2), a gabled roof (C3), of thick slate (D3), to have tall windows (E6), with vertically sliding sashes (F8), a doorway with a renaissance type surround (G5), be two-storey (H4), to have the two unit and cross-passage plan (J4) and to have a barn attached, laithe-house fashion (K7).

217

	1	2	3	4	5	6	7	8	9	0
A walling	stone	brick	Flint, cobble &c.	clay, cob &c.	half-timber	tile & math tile	plaster	weather board	others in each group	none applicable
B w.technique	solid wall rendered	mixture of materials	irregular, e.g. random rubble	regular, e.g. knapped flint	clay lump	square panels	tall panels	interrupted cill		
C roof shape	hipped	gablet	gabled	half-hipped	h-hipped and gablet	gambrel	M-shaped	single pitch		
D r.materials	thatch	fan slate	thick slate	plain tile	pantile	stone flags	stone tiles	combination		
E windows	lancet	transomed	mullioned	square	elongated	tall	multiple	revival		

Diagram for coded description. Sheet 1.

Diagram for coded description. Sheet 2.

	1	2	3	4	5	6	7	8	9 others in each group	0 none applicable
F w.frames	unglazed, iron bars	leaded light	mullioned, unglazed	w.i. side-hung casements	wooden, side hung c'ment	Fixed light, opening vent.	horizontally sliding sash	vertically sliding sash		
G doorways	pointed arch	4-centred arch	square head	decorated lintel	ren. surround	Semi-circular arch	revival details	heavy wood frame		
H sections	one storey	one storey & 2 storey wing	one and a half storey	two storey	two and a half storey	three storey	three and a half	tower house		
I plans	First Floor open hall	ground floor open hall	two-unit	two-unit and cross-passage	inside cross passage	central Fire-places	double-pile	double-pile single-fronted		
J links	individual house	attached to one house	part of a row	house over house	back to back house	longhouse type	lathe-house type	part of mill &c		

219

c) Intensive Survey

During the progress of an extensive survey, it will be seen that certain building forms recur even in the most picturesque village of apparently haphazard development as typical of a certain period or a certain level of society. Examples of such buildings should be selected for intensive study through the preparation of measured drawings. This is a procedure which requires comparatively little skill or experience providing it is done in a systematic way. The refinements of the measuring procedure and the separate procedure of drawing out from measured notes may be discovered from one of the several books on draughtsmanship available but an outline here of the basic points may prove useful.

There are two distinct processes involved; measuring and drawing these should ideally, but not essentially, be carried out by the same person and as soon as possible after each other.

A. MEASURING

1. *Personnel.* An ideal team is three; one surveyor and two helpers.

2. *Equipment.* (Metric equivalents in brackets). A hardbacked pad preferably of foolscap/A4 size, a cloth tape 66 ft. long (20 m.), an extending rod 6 ft. long (2 m.), a spring steel tape 6ft. (2 m.) long, a simple weight and cord for a plumb line, a ball of plasticene, a camera with black-and-white film, a flashlight, pencils, and coloured ball-point pens.

3. *Procedure*

(*a*) prepare sketch plans, sections, and elevations. These should be reasonably in proportion but should not attempt to show too much detail.

(*b*) prepare larger scale details in plan, section, and elevation, using the sketch plans as a key and with cross-referencing.

(*c*) locate the building by triangulation from some base line, e.g. the front fence.

(*d*) proceed from room to room, take plan dimensions, including diagonals, and of rough openings, e.g. window jamb to jamb, ignoring window frames.

(*e*) take sectional dimensions using staircases to give overall heights, floor to ceiling heights for separate rooms, roof space for accessible roof construction, and angle of roof slope.

(*f*) take dimensions of each elevation in turn. These should be related to a horizontal datum line (e.g. top of a plinth) not the varying ground line. At upper levels dimensions may have to be taken from open windows. In the absence of long ladders, dimensions of chimney stacks may have to be estimated e.g. by counting brick courses.

(*g*) take dimensions of selected details.

(*h*) take photographs of elevations and details; a composite photograph may be useful on a cramped site.

4. *Taking and noting dimensions.* With a team of three, one helper should hold the fixed end of the tape, another should read off each dimension and the surveyor should book down on his pad. Running dimensions are to be preferred wherever possible (see diagram), and using a long run through doors, to take in several rooms, as a check. It will be helpful if the sketch plans are drawn in pencil, dimensions and dimension lines shown in some other colour and notes and cross references in other colours.

5. *Assembling the survey notes.* To avoid subsequent confusion, each separate sheet should bear the address of the building, the name of the surveyor, the date of survey, and a number (e.g. sheet 1 of 10).

B. DRAWING

1. *Personnel.* Although the measured notes should be prepared in such a way that anyone could draw them out, it is obviously preferable that the surveyor draws them, and when his memory is fresh.

2. *Equipment.* A drawing board, which need only be a piece of blockboard with 'formica' on one face and two adjacent edges, a simple T-square, an adjustable set-square, masking tape to hold the paper, good quality tracing paper, a Rexel type pencil with 4H and 2H leads, a soft eraser, an architectural scale divided into divisions of $\frac{1}{4}$ in., $\frac{1}{8}$ in. etc. (1:50, 1:100 etc.), an ink pen and a selection of removable nibs (e.g. on the 'Graphos' or the 'Rapidograph' principle), a pair of simple ink and pencil springbow compasses.

3. *Procedure*

(*a*) Choose a scale for each part of the drawing. This should be aproppriate to the subject and to the possibility of reproduction. For most vernacular buildings, plans and elevations drawn out to a scale of $\frac{1}{8}$ in. to the foot (1:100) with sections at $\frac{1}{4}$ in. to the foot (1:50) and details of windows etc. to $\frac{1}{2}$ in. or 1 in. to the foot (1:25 or 1:10) and site plans at $\frac{1}{8}$ in. (1:100) scale, will give the appropriate amount of detail and be suitable for reductions in block-making.

(*b*) Set out the various sheets using overall dimensions as a guide. It is customary to arrange a site plan with north at the top, the floor plans with the main entrance facing the bottom of the sheet and the main elevation above the ground floor plan.

(*c*) Set out in pencil each part of the drawing using the compasses to establish triangulation. Running dimensions will be helpful in using the scale. If several parts of the drawing are worked up simultaneously mistakes can be found and corrected without too much waste of effort.

(*d*) When the whole of the work has been completed in pencil it should be inked in, using varying thicknesses for lines of varying importance.

(*e*) Lettering should then be added. Hand script is no longer fashionable but stencil or transfer lettering is readily available and easy to use.

(*f*) Finally, each sheet should be given a title and date, north points should be provided for the plans and written and drawn scales in both Imperial and metric measure included.

4. *Draughtsmanship*

(*a*) The drawings are intended to communicate information. To this end the presence or absence of any line is significant and its thickness should be in relation to its importance. A plan is a horizontal section, the most important line being that which indicates the cut through the wall, within that cut line no information is available, and none should be invented. Looking downwards, the walls as seen at windows, the steps at the door, the hearth, and any changes of level are important. Less important are lines indicating window frames, glass lines, fixed furniture, etc. Least important are lines indicating a floor pattern or material texture. Similar considerations apply to sections. In elevations the silhouette lines are most important, with openings, changes of plane, and jointing in decreasing order.

(*b*) Records of fact and items of interpretation should be separated. Ideally one set of drawings should show what existed at the time of survey and another should be hatched to indicate assumed periods of construction, but the two sets are often combined.

(*Opposite*) A typical measured drawing of a vernacular building. Below is an example of the measured notes with indication of the way measurements are taken: running dimensions, diagonals, dimensions through openings to join rooms together, setbacks in recesses etc. Only a selection of the measurements is given.

GROUND FLOOR PLAN

FIRST FLOOR PLAN

SOUTH ELEVATION

WEST ELEVATION

FRONT DOOR

SECTION

WINDOW

223

d) Documentary Investigation

If it is the hope that careful examination of examples of vernacular architecture will help to illuminate the activities for which the buildings were intended and the processes by which they were brought into existence; it must equally be acknowledged that careful examination of documents relating to the buildings, their owners, and occupiers should help to elucidate some of the mysteries presented by the physical remains. Alongside the development of archaeological examination of the buildings the historians have adapted their own methods of inquiry to provide information at the vernacular level.

Ideally, of course, one would want to identify a specific building with the documents which relate to it. The obvious link should be the *title deeds* of the property. The present owners may only have a recent summary of the various conveyances, but sometimes the archives of a local Solicitor, or a County Record Office can supply more complete deeds. These, however, relating to the land, will rarely be of much direct value in connection with a building, but in giving a history of the ownership may tie down pieces of information. Sometimes in deeds of the late 18C. or 19C. a site plan is included; sometimes covenants or leases may be helpful.

In the absence of title deeds ownership or occupation may be established by reference to records of the *courts baron*, usually now held in a County Record Office, or to *surveys* made, often with maps, from time to time, and especially on change of ownership of an estate, to assist with administration. From the late 18C. onwards, *county directories* are very useful in relating people and occupations to addresses. *Glebe terriers* usually survive from about 1600 onwards and sometimes give quite detailed information on parsonage houses, their accommodation, building materials, and state of repair.

The various *taxation records* are useful in helping to give a general picture of a locality; but even when an individual piece of property can be identified the amount of actual information gained is not usually great. Nor can one expect any more reliable information to be volunteered by a property owner to a tax inspector in the past than at present. One very useful tax record, however, is the *tithe map*. These were prepared from about 1830 onwards and every Parish Church should possess a copy of the map for its parish. The tithe maps normally show and name each individual field and many picture quite reliably and sometimes quite delightfully separate houses and farm buildings. There is usually some indication of the crops grown in the field at the time of survey and this information helps to establish the use of various farm buildings. Maps prepared in connection with enclosure awards from about 1750 onwards, and of which a copy was originally held by the Parish, the Lord of the Manor and the Enclosure Commission may be helpful in identifying separate tenements and their owners at the time.

Having identified ownership of buildings, records may help to show how they were used. By far the most helpful documents in this respect are the inventories made by neighbours to help in establishing the estate of a deceased person. These probate inventories were made during the three centuries roughly from 1539 to 1839, but most survive from about 1650 onwards. They have been held in the various Diocesan Registries, but are, in most counties, being moved to the Record Office. The inventories vary a great deal in their completeness; some of them simply give a lump sum value to the moveable possessions of the deceased; but many list item by item and, systematically, room by room, the furniture, household equipment, farm animals, unconsumed fodder, farm implements, etc., as well as recording his monetary wealth.

For later periods, descriptions of buildings in general and their use may be made in the various *reports and surveys*. These include county reports to the Board of Agriculture, Prize Essays of the Royal Agricultural Society of England, contributions to the *Gentleman's Magazine*, the accounts of late 18C. and early 19C. travellers such as W. Pennant and Arthur Young as well as some of their predecessors like Celia Fiennes and William Harrison. Guide-book writers—such as Wordsworth—sometimes note the buildings half-hidden by the scenery; while observant clergymen, such as Rev. T. D. Whittaker of Whalley in Lancashire, provide information about the buildings of their parishes.

More detailed information on the buildings, their construction, and appearance, may be obtained from *building accounts* preserved with estate documents in agents' offices or in County Record Offices. Sometimes the accounts are set out in such a way that actual building quantities can be read off and an approximate size and form of the building deduced. Sometimes also diagrams or even plans accompany the accounts. Building contracts when surviving are less useful than might be expected, but until the general contractor emerged as an individual it was the practice for the building owner to let out contracts by trades and sometimes, (as does happen in the country at the present time) making no reference to the labour or materials he supplied himself.

Finally, *contemporary drawings and photographs* intended for other purposes must not be neglected for the sake of the vernacular buildings forming the topographical background.

Patience and persistence as well as a keen eye and a nose for detail are really essential in documentary investigation of vernacular buildings. Considerable effort with little reward is common experience and when effort is rewarded it is usually by an excess of information in one direction and scarcity in another. But even where actual identification of record and building cannot be made, the background information gained is quite unobtainable from the buildings themselves.

An attempt is made here to deduce the general lines of a house plan from the evidence given in an inventory, as affected by general knowledge of house types in that part of the country and of the early 18C.

It is assumed that the appraisers entered by the front door, turned right to the 'kitchen', then back along a lobby to the 'house' off which opened a 'dining room' and 'pantry'. They then retraced to the lobby, went downstairs to the cellar, then upstairs to the first floor where they visited, in the same order, the 'chambers' over kitchen, house and dining-room (this last also extending over the pantry); finally they ascended to the garrets. An idea of the dimensions of the house can be obtained from the furniture contained in the various rooms.

The information is, of course, limited and should be considered along-side other known information for someone of similar wealth and social status in a similar time and place.

AN INVENTORY OF THE GOODS OF MRS. PHILLIPSON &C OF THE TOWN OF ALMONDBURY IN THE COUNTY OF YORK DECEASED (1740)

	£ s. d.
Purse	1. 10. 0.

Goods in the Kitching

A Jack	12. 0.
A range end irons tongs coal rake fire point	15. 0.
A bakeing stone and cover 10s. 5 spits & rakes ⎫	
⎬	16. 6.
A fire shovel ⎭	
A tin(?) dripping Pan and standard 10s. a warming pan 3s.	13. 0.
Pot hooks a chopping bill a shreding Knife a brass ladle	2. 6.
2 iron pots three brass pans a bell a mortar & pestel	1. 18. 6.
2 sauce pans an iron bill 2 frying pans a toasting jack	7. 0.
2 water kits 1·6 an ax 3d. a stone 1s. a Draesar and case 4	6. 9.
4 chairs a buffet an oval table 10s. a bread creech 2	12. 6.

Goods in the House

7 chairs 14s. a craddle 2s an oval table 12 a long table 2s	1. 11. 0.
2 square tables 5 a range fire point and tongs and fire shovel 10	15. 0.
6 pictures 2 a fender 1·6 window curtains & rod 3	5. 6.

226

In the dining roome

A range tongs and fire shovel and point 4 a buffet 20s a glass 10	I. 14. 0.
in pewter 2. 10. 6 chairs 12s and oval table 12	3. 14. 0.
a square table a little oval table 3s 5 pictures 5s	8. 0.
12 pictures 6s window curtains and rod 7s and 10 cushions	18. 0.
4 Candlesticks and snuffers 7s a coffee pot 3s a box 6	10. 6.

In the pantery

A chest 5 6 barrels 6s Delf and case 6s a cupboard 4	I. I. 0.
a napkin press a kneading kit a stand 1	2. 0.

In the Cellar

A stone and stand 2·6 1 Barrel 1s a Salting fat	6. 6.

In the kitching chamber

A bed and bedding £4.4. in silver plate 2.10	6. 14. 0.
A pair of chest of drawers and a box	I. I. 0.
A desk and frame 2s	2. 0.

In the house chamber

A bed and bedding £4.4. in silver Plate 2.10	6. 14. 0.
A pair chest of drawers 15s a coach chair 10s three chairs 3	I. 8. 0.
Window curtains and rods 5s a table and range 3s and a glass 2	10. 0.
Linnen	I. 0. 0.

In the dining Roome chamber

Bed and Bedding 4 1 pair chest of drawers 1.1 2 tables 4s	5. 5. 0.
5 chairs 2 buffets a Range a tea table	16. 0.
A parcel of glasses and delf 3s a standard 1s	4. 0.
A press bed and close stool 10 a quilting frame 6	10. 0.

In the garrets

3 chests 18 3 wheelers 2 a pair bedstocks 2 bottles	I. 8. 0.
A pull of slate and laths 3s a stone trough	5. 0.
The hustements in an about the house	5. 0.
	£37. 7. 0.

(*from. p.* 202 *Transac. Cumb. & Westm. Antiq. and Arch. Soc. N.S.* 64, 1964, *article on the Phillipson family by T. G. Fahy*)

APPENDIX 2.   Glossary Notes

In the hope that the various illustrations and captions will serve to illustrate the terms commonly used in the study of vernacular architecture no separate glossary has been prepared.

For architectural terms used in both vernacular and polite architecture the *Illustrated Glossary of Architecture, 850–1830* by John Harris and Jill Lever, Faber and Faber, 1966 is useful. More specialized illustrated glossaries appear in R. W. Brunskill, *Timber Building in Britain*, Gollancz, 1985, for example. However two sets of glossary notes are included here: one is a summary of room names used in the past (a full glossary by M. W. Barley appears as Chapter XX in 1. Ll. Foster and L. Alcock, *Culture and Environment*, Routledge and Kegan Paul, 1963); the other is a standard set of terms for use in the study of farm buildings based on one originally prepared by J. E. C. Peters.

ROOM NAMES

Buttery   Essentially a cool storage space; during the 16C. and 17C. a common term for the place in which drink was kept.

Cellar   A storage room but on the ground floor unless stated otherwise.

Chamber   A general-purpose room name, supplanted in the 17C. by the term 'room'; in the South of England it meant at first a ground-floor room for sleeping; first-floor chambers used for sleeping were found from later 16C. onwards; sometimes a distinction was made between upstairs store-chambers and upstairs bed-chambers. A chamber might also be used for cottage industry.

Dairy   This term as well as *milk-house* was used to refer to a place for the storage and processing of milk but in smaller houses in the late 17C. it might refer to the only service room in a house.

Hall   Strictly speaking the term is now used for a room open to the roof and normally on the ground floor but it was formerly the usual word for a living room except in parts of the North of England.

House   As well as its modern meaning of a dwelling the term was used in Yorkshire and some other parts of the North of England as a general term for enclosing structure thus *calf-house, cow-house, dwelling-house*. It was also used for the principal living room as *house, house-body, house-part* etc. The *fire-house* might be either the living room or the complete dwelling.

Kitchen   Cooking was not necessarily done in the kitchen nor was that necessarily devoted solely to cooking; the kitchen might be a detached

228

structure; the term was also used, especially in the 19C. in the North of England for the principal living room of a house.

Parlour Always a ground-floor room and usually at the superior end of the hall; in the South usually denoted a sitting room, elsewhere a room primarily for sleeping. The term *bower* was used by Chaucer and remained in use in Cumbria through the 18C.

Solar (Soller) Found in East Anglia as a first-floor room.

FARM BUILDING TERMS

1. *Barn* Building in which hay, corn or straw is stored, usually with a threshing floor. The barn may incorporate other accommodation e.g. stable.

1a. *Bank Barn* Barn at 1st floor level, usually parallel to slope, entered at ground level or from a ramp; has stable, cow house, cartshed, etc., below.

1b. *Hay Barn* A special type of barn, lacking a threshing floor, usually with open walls, intended only for storage of hay.

2. *Bays* Part of barn, divided by trusses or partial divisions, may be at ground or first floor level.

3. *Cartshed* Building for housing carts and implements, usually open fronted.

3a. *Traphouse (wainhouse)* As cartshed but for trap, gig, coach, etc.

4. *Corn* The name given in any region for the principal local grain crop, e.g. rye, wheat, oats, barley, maize, in unthreshed state, whether cut or growing in field.

5. *Chaff* Husks of grain removed at winnowing, or hay or straw cut into short lengths.

6. *Cow house* (byre, shippon, mistal, cow-shed etc.) Building in which cattle are kept tied, not loose.

7. *Farmstead* Farm buildings and house as a group.

8. *Field Barn* Isolated cow-house or shelter shed, usually with a loft over.

9. *Foldyard* Open yard in which livestock are free to move about.

10. *Grain* Threshed ears of corn.

11. *Granary* Room in which grain is stored, whether in sacks or bulk. Not a corn hole, which is a small room opening off the threshing floor for temporary storage of threshed grain, but includes a building raised on staddle stones.

12. *Hay* Cut and dried grass.

13. *Horse engine* (gin, ginny ring) Horse-driven source of rotary power.

13a. *Horse engine house* (gin gang, gin case) Building to house horse engine.

14. *Loft* Upper floor room or floored space in roof, usually associated with barn, cow-house, or stable, may have open walls.

15. *Loose box* Separate compartment for livestock free to move about.

16. *Manger* Trough for food for livestock, irrespective of height above ground: not a rack.

17. *Partition* Division between stalls.

18. *Pigsty*   Building for pigs, small room with adjoining yard.
19. *Pitch hole (pitching eye)*   Opening in wall, usually of barn or loft, for unloading corn, hay or straw, usually closed by sliding or hinged shutter, may be square, circular or rectangular.
20. *Rack*   Frame of wood or iron to hold hay or straw for feeding livestock.
21. *Shelter shed (hovel)*   Completely or partially open fronted building for loose cattle, horses or sheep, free to enter or leave at will.
22. *Stable*   Building in which horses are tied.
22a. *Hackney stable*   Stable for riding horses or those for pulling gig, coach, etc.
22b. *Wagon stable*   Stable for working horses.
23. *Stall*   Standing place for animal when tied.
24. *Straw*   Stem of corn after threshing.
25. *Threshing Floor*   The part of a barn, paved or boarded, on which corn was threshed by hand flailing.

Initial Example Reconsidered

This shows items which have been observed in the order in which comments appear in this handbook: walling material and construction, roof shape and materials, plan and sectional form, window and door details, and relation to farm buildings.

Fan-isaf, Merthyr Cynog, Breconshire

External Details

a. sandstone random rubble, irregular shape, wide joints, widely spread mortar, quoins not stressed, colourwashed overall.
b. gabled roof
c. plain close verge,
d. plain close eaves, cast iron rain water goods added,
e. roof at present of Welsh Slate, regular courses, thin slates, steep pitch (over 45°) suggests replacement of thatch
f. tile ridge
g. chimneys at each gable, plain square stacks, one larger than the other
h. water tabling remains to protect junction with lower roof
i. three dormers, all entirely in roof space, Welsh Slate roofs and cheeks, tile ridges, wooden barge boards, in present form probably date from re-roofing in slate.
j. plan form: basically two-unit, subsidiary unit divided between parlour and pantry
k. sectional form: basically one storey with a continuous loft, this loft now lit by prominent dormer windows
l. present straight flight staircase, originally probably spiral alongside fireplace, no window or other outside indication.
m. window shape: essentially squarish, wooden lintels, no architraves
n. window frames, probably vertically sliding sash, may have been renewed
o. door shape, no dressings

p. door details, simple four panelled door in conventional door frame
q. farm building attached at lower end, no sign of intercommunication, plinth stones run through, straight joint above, farm buildings may have been rebuilt and possibly heightened, roof pitch lower, more consistent with slate covering
r. attached cow house

Sketch Plan
1. hall, 2. parlour, 3. pantry, 4. former stair? 5. later scullery, 6. possible stable, 7. cow house with central feeding passage, loft above, 8. calf pen, 9. loose box, 10. barn, two-storage bays each side of, 11. threshing floor, 12. cart shed below, granary above, internal wooden staircase access, 13. garden, 14. orchard, 15. foldyard.

(based partly on sketch plans by S. R. Jones, extended by R.W.B. on the site, July 1967)

NOTES, REFERENCES AND RECOMMENDATIONS FOR FURTHER READING

Introduction

a. *General Bibliography*. One of the main activities of the Vernacular Architecture Group has been the preparation of bibliographies on the various aspects of the subject. These have been published as one volume: *A Bibliography on Vernacular Architecture*, edited by Sir Robert de Z. Hall and published by David and Charles in 1972. Supplements edited by D. J. Michelmore are issued by the Vernacular Architecture Group from time to time.

The following list of general, regional and local works includes those which are generally available (in libraries at least, as some are out of print) and which have been particularly useful in the preparation of the various editions of this book.

General Books (though many with regional sections)

Addy, S. O., *The Evolution of the English House*, 1898, 2nd ed. revised by Sir John Summerson, 1933—still a basic work though the author's views on the link between British and German plans and on the particular significance of certain measurements related to house plans are no longer generally accepted.

Ayres, J., *The Shell Book of the Home in Britain*, Faber and Faber, 1981—deals with the decoration, design, and interiors generally of vernacular houses and cottages 1500–1850.

Barley, M. W., *The English Farmhouse and Cottage*, Routledge and Kegan Paul, 1961—still one of the most valuable works on the subject, based on both field and documentary investigation; covers mainly the period 1550–1700 but with links back to medieval precedents.

Barley, M. W., *Houses and History*, Faber and Faber, 1986.

Batsford, H., and Fry, C., *The English Cottage*, Batsford, 1938—still useful as a record of buildings, many of which have now disappeared or been altered out of recognition.

Briggs, M. S., *The English Farmhouse*, Batsford, 1953—includes some houses which are not strictly farmhouses, but also includes information on 19C. farmstead layouts.

Brunskill, R. W., *Houses*, Collins Archaeology, 1982 —describes and illustrates type plans of urban and rural houses and cottages.

Clifton-Taylor, A., *The Pattern of English Building*, Faber and Faber, 1972—deals comprehensively and with many illustrations with walling and roofing materials, mainly, but not entirely, as found in vernacular buildings.

Hoskins, W. G., *Provincial England*, Macmillan, 1963—collected essays including the important *Rebuilding of Rural England 1570–1640*.

Innocent, C. F., *The Development of English Building Construction*, Cambridge University Press, 1916, re-issued with an introduction by Sir Robert de Z. Hall, 1975—has yet to be superseded as a general book on vernacular building construction, though, based mainly on evidence from Northern England, appears rather ill-balanced.

Jones, S. R., *English Village Homes*, Batsford, 1936—like Batsford and Fry includes many useful photographs and drawings.

Lloyd, N., *History of the English House*, Architectural Press, 1931, re-issued 1975—puts some vernacular houses in a wider context.

Mercer, E., *English Vernacular Houses*, HMSO, 1975—an authoritative work comprising an inventory of some 500 examples, a detailed commentary and many plans and photographs.

Peate, I. C., *The Welsh House*, Brython Press, 1940, 2nd ed. 1946—a pioneering work dealing with houses as an aspect of folk culture.

Penoyre, J. and J., *Houses in the Landscape*, Faber and Faber, 1978—includes many photographs and regional maps of building materials.

Potter, M. and A., *Houses*, John Murray, 3rd ed., 1973—brief summary well illustrated by drawings.

Prizeman, J., *Your House, The Outside View*, Hutchinson, 1975—has many coloured illustrations.

Salzman, L. F., *Building in England down to 1540*, Oxford University Press, 1952—based on documents and though dealing mainly with the superior architecture of the medieval period has much on vernacular building.

Smith, P., *Houses of the Welsh Countryside*, HMSO, 1975—this is the definitive work on its subject and has many plans, sketches, maps and other illustrations.

Thirsk, J., (ed.), *The Agrarian History of England and Wales*, Vol. IV, 1500–1640, Cambridge University Press, 1967—among the many relevant contributions are important ones by M. W. Barley and P. Smith on English and Welsh houses respectively; their accounts have been extended in Vol. V(ii).

Wood, M. E., *The English Medieval House*, Dent, 1965, re-issued 1981 by Ferndale Editions—mainly superior architecture but does extend into the vernacular range.

Regional Books (though many contain sections of general significance)

Brunskill, R.W., *Vernacular Architecture of the Lake Counties*, Faber and Faber, 1974—deals with the present Cumbria incorporating Cumberland, Westmorland and Lancashire north of the Sands.

Caffyn, L., *Workers' Housing in West Yorkshire, 1750–1920*, HMSO, 1986—deals with cottages of urban and rural industrial workers.

Chesher, V. M. and F. J., *The Cornishman's House*, D. Bradford Barton, 1968—Cornwall, mainly medieval to 17C.

Fox, Sir Cyril, and Lord Raglan, *Monmouthshire Houses*, National Museum of Wales, 3 vols., 1951–4—upland Monmouthshire; established procedures and dating criteria folowed by many later scholars.

Giles, C., *Rural Houses of West Yorkshire, 1400–1830*, HMSO, 1986—deals with houses of various sizes outside the developing towns.

Hall, L., *The Rural Houses of North Avon and South Gloucestershire, 1400–1720*, Bristol City Library, 1983—detailed study of houses in parts of Somerset and Gloucestershire.

Harrison, B., and Hutton, B., *Vernacular Houses in North Yorkshire and Cleveland*, J. Donald, 1984—a comprehensive study of a large part of Yorkshire.

Jones, S. R., and Smith, J. T., 'The Houses of Breconshire', Parts 1 to 5, appeared in issues of *Brycheiniog* from 1963 on—a very full study of the houses of nearly the whole of the county.

Lowe, J., *Welsh Country Workers' Housing 1775–1875*, National Museum of Wales, Cardiff, 1985.

Mason, R. T., *Framed Buildings of the Weald*, published by the author, 1964—a study of typical houses of parts of Kent and Sussex.

Nevill, R., *Old Cottages and Domestic Architecture in South-West Surrey*, 1889—this was the first regional study and established principles which have been followed in many subsequent studies.

Pearson, S., *Rural Houses of the Lancashire Pennines, 1560–1760*, HMSO, 1985—deals with the period in which great prosperity in north-east Lancashire was reflected in house design.

Royal Commission on the Ancient and Historical Monuments of Wales, *Inventories*, HMSO—the various county inventories have devoted an increasing proportion of their space to vernacular buildings; those of Anglesey, Caernarvonshire and Glamorgan (forthcoming) are especially useful.

Royal Commission on the Historical Monuments of England, *Inventories*, HMSO—again, the most recent county inventories include much on vernacular architecture; those of Dorset and Cambridgeshire are most useful for rural vernacular and York, Salisbury and Stamford for urban vernacular.

Sandon, E., *Suffolk Houses*, Baron, 1977—covers Great Houses as well as vernacular.

Walton, J., *Homesteads of the Yorkshire Dales*, Dalesman Publishing Co., 1947—an early booklet introducing the subject though now largely superseded by Harrison and Hutton, 1984.

Wood-Jones, R. B., *Traditional Domestic Architecture of the Banbury Region*, Manchester University Press, 1963—deals with part of Oxfordshire and adjacent counties; for over twenty years was quite the most comprehensive regional study published in England.

District and Local Books (though often containing material of regional significance)

Thorough studies of the vernacular architecture of a single parish or a small number of parishes are now being published, usually by local societies or the extra-mural departments of universities. Examples include the following:

Alcock, N. W., *Stoneleigh Villagers*, University of Warwick Open Studies, 1978

Harding, J. M., *Four Centuries of Charlwood Houses*, Charlwood Society (Surrey), 1976.

Hutton, B., (ed.), *Hatfield and its People*, Hatfield WEA (Herts.), 1963.

Lacey, H. M. and U. E., *The Timber-framed Buildings of Steyning*, Worthing (Sussex), 1974.

Machin, R., *The Houses of Yetminster*, University of Bristol Extra-Mural Dept. (Dorset), 1978.

Martin D., and Mastin, B., *An Architectural History of Robertsbridge*, Hastings Area Archaeological Papers (Sussex), 1974.

Somerset and South Avon Vernacular Building Research Group, *Somerset Villages, The Vernacular Buildings of West and Middle Chinnock*, Glastonbury, Somerset, 1984.

Wade, J., (ed.), *Traditional Kent Buildings*, series published by Canterbury College of Art, 1980 on—measured drawings of various buildings.

Walton, J., *Early Timbered Buildings of the Huddersfield District*, Tolson Memorial Museum, Huddersfield, 1955—a pioneering work still of interest.

Watson, R. C., and McClintock, M. E., *Traditional Houses of the Fylde*, Centre for North-West Regional Studies, University of Lancaster, 1979.

The Setting for Vernacular Buildings

Many books have recently been published as a result of the interest in local history and of the history of the landscape; three only are mentioned:

Hoskins, W. G., *The Making of the English Landscape*, Penguin, 1970—first published in 1955 this has been a most influential book.

Roberts, B. K., *The Making of the English Village*, Longman, 1986—will develop from Dr. Roberts many articles on the subject.

Taylor, C., *Village and Farmstead: History of Rural Settlement*, Phillips, 1983—authoritative and well illustrated.

Vernacular Buildings in a World Setting

Most European countries and many countries in other parts of the world have developed studies in vernacular architecture and primitive building, sometimes as part of folk life studies, sometimes by way of archaeology, history or geology, sometimes out of a feeling of nationalism. Rather than single out any country the following general works are mentioned:

Oliver P., (ed.), *Shelter and Society*, Barrie and Jenkins, 1969—contains a thoughtful introduction and contributions about several countries.

Rapaport, A., *House Form and Culture*, Prentice Hall, 1969,—looks at the subject on a world scale and distinguishes between the primitive, the vernacular and the academic traditions.

Rudofsky, B., *Architecture without Architects*, Museum of Modern Art, New York, 1964—originally prepared for an exhibition, this has been an influential book, though no examples are taken from Britain.

Periodicals

Vernacular Architecture (henceforth *VA*), the journal of the Vernacular Architecture Group, has been published annually since 1970 and is exclusively devoted to the subject. Articles on vernacular architecture appear in the journals or transactions of such national organizations as the Ancient Monuments Society, the British Archaeological Association, the Royal Archaeological Institute, the Society for Medieval Archaeology, the Society for Post-Medieval Archaeology and the Society for Folk Life Studies. In addition articles on subjects of local or regional interest usually appear in the transactions of the appropriate county archaeological society. The monthly magazines *Period Home* and *Traditional Homes* often include material of interest in the study of vernacular buildings.

Theses and Dissertations

Many PhD, MA, MPhil and BA theses and dissertations have been completed or are in progress. Some were listed in *VA*, Vol. 14, 1983 and others may be found in the *Research Register* of the Society of Architectural Historians.

National Monuments Records and Statutory Lists

The National Monuments Records for England, Wales and Scotland are maintained in London, Aberystwyth and Edinburgh at the headquarters of the various Royal Commissions on Historical Monuments. All include many valuable records of vernacular buildings as well as others while the National Monuments Record for England incorporates a large and rapidly increasing collection of reports on vernacular buildings which include measured drawings.

The statutory *lists* of buildings of 'special architectural or historical interest' were first compiled as an aid to local planning authorities by way of the Town and Country Planning Act, 1947. They have been amplified from time to time and the current re-survey is likely to bring the total for England alone to some 500,000 buildings of which a large proportion are likely to be works of vernacular architecture. The *List Descriptions* are now quite extensive for each building. Parish lists may be consulted at the offices of the relevant local planning authority and at the National Monuments Record offices.

Sites and Monuments Records are being developed in most counties. Although originally intended to record antiquities most now include many vernacular buildings. In some counties the Records are part of the County Planning Department, in others part of the Archives or Record Office and in some counties they may be part of the Library and Museum Service.

b. Size-Types. The four size-types were distinguished by Professor R. A. Cordingley in his contribution to Section H of the 1948 meeting of the British Association for the Advancement of Science and described under the heading 'Rural House Types' on pp. 23–4 of the *Proceedings* of the Association for that year.

c. The Vernacular Zone. The Great Rebuilding was described by W. G. Hoskins in his article 'The Rebuilding of Rural England, 1570–1640' which

236

first appeared in *Past and Present* for November 1953 and was reprinted in Hoskins' *Provincial England*, 1963. The symbols in the diagram of the vernacular zone refer to dated vernacular buildings illustrated in the books listed below or taken from my own records: M. W. Barley, 1961; N. Lloyd, 1931; P. Smith in Thirsk (ed.), 1967; R. B. Wood-Jones, 1963. An article by R. Machin, 'The Great Rebuilding: a reassessment' in *Past and Present*, No. 77, Nov. 1977, suggests modifications to Hoskins' argument. Harrison and Hutton, 1984, question the idea of the Great Rebuilding. S. Wrathmell shares the doubts in 'The Vernacular Threshold of Northern Peasant Houses', *VA*, Vol. 15, 1984, but suggests that 'from the thirteenth century to the seventeenth century the peasant farmers of Northumberland constructed low-cost buildings which would stand for centuries provided that they were subject to a high degree of maintenance and repair'. It appears that they were succeeded by 'permanent dwellings which involved high cost and a low level of maintenance'. This seems very like a Great Rebuilding. The thesis is also supported by N. W. Alcock, 'The Great Rebuilding and its Later Stages'. *VA*, Vol. 14, 1983.

To repeat the argument put forward here: even the most casual observation of houses in England and Wales, at least, shows that from a date which varies with status and place substantially constructed houses survive. These houses may incorporate parts of their predecessors. They may be succeeded by other newly built houses. They may themselves display additions, modifications, items of modernization since their first substantial construction. They may repeat the plans of their predecessors because change of building material and methods of construction do not necessarily imply change of plan. The reasons for this substantial rebuilding may be many and may vary with circumstance, place and time: for instance earlier building might be structurally inadequate through short-lived materials, might require too much maintenance, there might be materials or constructional methods which were now available (such as the supply of bricks and tiles), there might be a sudden increase in prosperity which allowed money to be invested in rebuilding, there might be a change in tenure which justified investment in expensive buildings of indefinite life. As we discover more about the process of providing vernacular buildings we will understand why such a rebuilding took place but it is too early to deny that something recognizable as a vernacular threshold does exist.

d. Organization of the Book. This handbook concentrates on the vernacular architecture of England and Wales. There is a different tradition in Scotland which is briefly noted. Ireland has different traditions again, mentioned but not discussed here.

The traditional county names and imperial measure have been retained in the text.

WALLING

a. General. The distinction between the different walling and cladding materials follows that made by R. A. Cordingley and described and illus-

237

trated by R. W. Brunskill in 'A Systematic Procedure for Recording English Vernacular Architecture', *Transactions of the Ancient Monuments Society* (henceforth *TAMS*), Vol. 13, 1965–6. Distribution maps showing the use of the various materials have been placed together in Chapter 8 to help comparisons.

b. Stone, Irregular and Regular, Pebble, Cobble and Flint. The chapters in A. Clifton-Taylor, 1972, have been expanded in A. Clifton-Taylor and A. S. Ireson, *English Stone Building*, Gollancz, 1983. Further information on e.g. masonry walling techniques may be found in the older text books of building construction such as W. B. Mackay, *Building Construction*, Vols. I, II, III, Longmans, 1938 on, and in the pre-war editions of *Mitchell's Building Construction*. There is a brief note on watershot stonework in the Pennines by F. Atkinson in *Transactions of the Lancs. and Chesh. Antiq. Soc.*, Vol. 59, 1959.

c. Brick Walling. The original work on the subject is N. Lloyd, *A History of English Brickwork*, H. G. Montgomery, 1925; many of the examples are of polite rather than vernacular architecture and later research has qualified some of the conclusions. More generally available are *English Brickwork* by R. W. Brunskill and A. Clifton-Taylor, Ward Lock, 1977 (which includes an illustrated glossary) and *Bricks to Build a House*, by J. Woodforde, Routledge and Kegan Paul, 1976. Jane A. Wight, *Brick Building in England*, John Baker, 1972, deals with the period Middle Ages to 1550 but mainly in superior buildings. Dr. A Brian's two articles include fascinating distribution maps (though, again, they are not confined to vernacular brickwork): 'A Regional Survey of Brick Bonding in England and Wales', *VA*, Vol. 3, 1972 and Vol. 11, 1980. Much new material is appearing in the *Bulletin of the British Brick Society* edited by T. P. Smith who has also prepared a provisional bibliography for that society.

d. Earth Walling. A good general introduction is provided by J. McCann, *Clay and Cob Buildings*, Shire, 1983, and a more technical introduction by J. R. Harrison in 'The Mud Wall in England', *TAMS*, Vol. 28, 1984. The various local techniques have been the subject of articles which include the following: R. W. Brunskill, 'Clay Construction in Cumberland', *TAMS*, Vol. 10, 1962; K. Hodgson, C. M. L. Bouch, C. G. Bulman, 'Lamonby Farm, Burgh-by-Sands, Cumberland', *Trans. Cumb. and Westm. Antiq. and Arch. Soc.*, Vol. 53, 1954; M. Seaborne, 'Cob Cottages in Northants', *Northamptonshire Past and Present*, Vol. 3, no. 5, 1964. Comparable Irish techniques are noted in K. Danaher, 'Materials and Methods in Irish Traditional Building', *Journal of the Royal Society of Antiquaries of Ireland*, Vol. 88, 1957, and in A. Gailey, *Rural Houses of the North of Ireland*, J. Donald, 1984. Comparative Scottish techniques are described in A. Fenton, 'Stone and Turf Walling', *Folk Life*, Vol. 6, 1968. Some historical material was included in C. Williams-Ellis, *Building in Cob, Pisé and Stabilized Earth*, 1947.

e. Timber Frame Construction. An excellent basic introduction to the subject is provided by R. Harris, *Discovering Timber-Framed Buildings*, Shire, 1978.

238

More introductory material including an extensive illustrated glossary appears in R. W. Brunskill, *Timber Building in Britain*, Gollancz, 1985. Major works incorporating research over many decades include F. W. B. Charles, *Medieval Cruck Building and its Derivatives*, Society for Post-Medieval Archaeology, 1967, and the historical parts of F. W. B. and M. Charles, *Conservation of Timber Buildings*, Hutchinson, 1984, while the works of C. A. Hewett include the indispensable *English Historic Carpentry*, Phillimore, 1980, as well as two books which deal mainly with the carpentry of superior rather than vernacular buildings: *Church Carpentry. A Study Based on Essex Examples*, Phillimore, 1982 and *English Cathedral and Monastic Carpentry*, 1985. N. W. Alcock (ed.), *Cruck Construction: an Introduction and Catalogue*, CBA Research Report No. 42, 1982, superseded Dr. Alcock's *Cruck Catalogue* of 1973 and extends his work by including contributions by others on various aspects of the subject.

Among local publications that by H. M. and U. E. Lacey, 1974, has already been listed; another example is P. F. Ryder, *Timber-Framed Building in South Yorkshire*, South Yorks. County Council, n.d., c. 1978.

In recent years many articles on timber-frame construction have been published in national and county journals. The following selection includes many useful in the study of vernacular architecture:

Charles, F. W. B., 'Post construction and the rafter roof', *VA*, Vol. 10, 1979—suggests possible origins for some features of timber-frame construction.

Cordingley, R. A., 'British Historical Roof-Types and their Members', *TAMS*, Vol. 9, 1961—a detailed description and classification of roof trusses together with a glossary.

Gee, E. A., 'The Chronology of Crucks', *TAMS*, Vol. 22, 1977—helps in the difficult matter of attempting to date cruck-built structures.

Rigold, S. E., 'Timber-framed building at Steventon, Berkshire', *Transactions of the Newbury and District Field Club*, Vol. 10, No. 4, 1958.

Smith, J. T., 'Medieval Roofs: a Classification', *Archaeological Journal*, Vol. 115, 1960—introduced theories, terms and methods of study which are still generally accepted.

Smith, J. T., 'Cruck Construction, a Survey of the Problems', *Medieval Archaeology*, Vol. 8, 1964—another pioneering work of fundamental importance.

Smith, J. T., 'Timber-framed building in England', *Archaeological Journal*, Vol. 122, 1966—extensively illustrated by drawings and maps; the distinction in wall framing noted here and illustrated in a general way in the distribution map is based on this article.

Smith, J. T. 'The Early Development of Timber Building: the passing brace and reversed assembly', *Archaeological Journal*, Vol. 131, 1974—deals with the introduction of techniques from which conventional timber framing developed.

Webster, V. R., 'Cruck-framed buildings in Leicestershire', *Transactions of the Leicestershire Archaeological Society*, Vol. 30, 1954.

Williams, E. H. D., 'Jointed crucks', *VA*, Vol. 8, 1977—deals with a technique which is localized but common in its locality.

f. Timber Walling and Cladding. Most of the references to timber-frame construction include details of the various half-timber and cladding techniques. However, mathematical tile cladding is attracting a literature of its own. The basic work remains A. Arschavir, 'False Fronts in Minor Domestic Architecture', *TAMS*, Vol. 4, 1956, but items have been corrected and the study brought up to date by M. Exwood in *Mathematical Tiles, Notes of Ewell Symposium*, 1981, and 'Mathematical Tiles', *VA*, Vol. 12, 1981, and by T. P. Smith in 'Re-facing with Brick-Tiles', *VA*, Vol. 10, 1979.

ROOFING

a. Generally. The classification and terminology used here is based on R. A. Cordingley, 1961. The reference given under *e. Timber Frame Construction* above generally apply to timber roofs on solid walls as well as those which are part of total timber-frame construction. Developments which took place as traditional construction was being superseded by scientific design are outlined by D. T. Yeomans in 'Historic development of timber structures', in J. Sunley and B. Bedding (eds.), *Timber in Construction*, Batsford, 1985.

b. Single and Double Rafter Roofs. In addition to the other references listed see J. M. Fletcher and P. S. Spokes, 'The origin and development of the Crown Post Roof', *Medieval Archaeology*, Vol. 8, 1964.

c. Thatched Roofing. The techniques still in use are thoroughly described and illustrated in Rural Industries Bureau, *The Thatcher's Craft*, published by the Bureau, 1961. See also M. Billet, *Thatching and Thatched Buildings*, Hale, 1979. For 'rafterless roofs', thatch carried on a roof-shaped heap of twigs, see J. E. C. Peters, 'The Solid Thatched Roof' in *VA*, Vol. 8, 1977, and D. M. Smith, 'Some Flat-roof Thatch Survivals', *Folk Life*, Vol. 16, 1978.

d. Stone Flags and Stone Tiles, including Horsham and Collyweston stone slates are described and illustrated in J. Walton, 'The English Stone-Slater's Craft', *Folk Life*, Vol. 13, 1975. There is also much on the subject in A. Clifton-Taylor and A. J. Ireson, 1983.

PLAN AND SECTIONAL FORM

a. Generally. The following are some of the works which include illustrations of the development of various forms of vernacular house plan: S. O. Addy, 1898 and 1933; N. W. Alcock series 'Devonshire Farmhouses' in *Transactions of the Devonshire Association*, from 1962 on; M. W. Barley, 1961; R. W. Brunskill, *Houses*, 1982; R. W. Brunskill, 'The Development of the Small House in the Eden Valley, 1650 to 1840', *Trans. Cumb. and Westm. Antiq. and Arch. Soc.*, Vol. 54, 1954; C. Carson, 'Segregation in Vernacular Buildings', *VA*, Vol. 7, 1976; P. A. Faulkner, 'Domestic Planning from the 12C. to the 14C.', *Archaeological Journal*, Vol. 115, 1960; Fox and Raglan, 1951 etc.; C. Giles, 1985; L. Hall, 1983; Harrison and Hutton, 1984; S. R. Jones and J. T. Smith, 1963 on; E. Mercer, 1975; S. Pearson, 1985; I. C. Peate, 1940 and 1946; M. E. Wood, 1965; R. B. Wood-Jones, 1963.

b. Planning Theory. J. M. Jenkins, 'Ground Rules of Welsh Houses: a Primary Analysis' in *Folk Life*, Vol. 5, 1967, suggests that the plan shapes of vernacular houses follow recognizable rules of proportion. Similar conclusions have followed study of American Small Houses and Cottages by A. J. Lawton, 'The Ground Rules of Folk Architecture', *Pennsylvania Folk Life*. In the American context planning theory has been taken still further in H. Glassie, *Folk Housing in Middle Virginia*, University of Tennessee, Knoxville, 1975.

c. Classifications. Various attempts at the classification of plan forms in different localities have been made; among the most systematic are: P. Eden, *Small Houses in England, 1520–1820*, Historical Association, 1969 which developed from that in the RCHM *Inventory for West Cambridgeshire*, 1968; and P. Smith, 1975, developing that produced for RCAHM (Wales) *Inventory for Caernarvonshire*, 1956–76. R. W. Brunskill, *Houses*, 1982, was written around classifications of rural and urban house plans and a development, *House and Cottages of Britain* is proposed for 1988 publication by Gollancz.

d. First Floor Family. Examples of tower-houses in part of England are described and illustrated in J. F. Curwen, *Castles and Towers of Cumberland, Westmorland and Lancashire North of the Sands*, Cumb. and Westm. Antiq. and Arch. Soc., 1913, re-issued 1965. More recent studies of examples in that region suggest that some towers were not self-contained houses but the surviving cross-wings of T-shaped or H-shaped houses; see G. Fairclough, 'Clifton Hall, Cumbria: Excavations 1977–79' and R. W. McDowall, 'Wraysholme Tower', in *Trans. Cumb. and Westm. Antiq. and Arch. Soc.*, Vols. 80, 1980, and 76, 1976 respectively.

Examples of first floor halls are described and illustrated in e.g. T. L. Marsden, 'The Manor House at Donington-le-Heath, *TAMS*, Vol. 10, 1962 and S. E. Rigold, 'Two Camerae of the Military Orders', *Archaeological Journal*, Vol. 122, 1966. For the special version known as the 'bastle house' see H. G. Ramm, R. W. McDowall and E. Mercer, *Shielings and Bastles*, HMSO, 1970 (though P. Dixon considers the term inappropriate as mentioned in his article 'Tower Houses, Pelehouses and Border Society', *Archaeological Journal*, Vol. 136, 1979).

e. The Hall Family. There are many articles on individual buildings of this type such as those published by R. T. Mason in *Sussex Archaeological Collections* and by E. W. Parkin in *Archaeologia Cantiana*, and a classic example is R. A. Cordingley and R. B. Wood-Jones on 'Chorley Hall', in *TAMS*, Vol. 7, 1959. For aisled halls see J. T. Smith, 'Medieval Aisled Halls', *Archaeological Journal*, Vol. 112, 1956 and 'A Fourteenth Century Aisled House, Edgars Farm Stowmarket', *Proceedings of the Suffolk Institute of Archaeology*, 1958. An interesting commentary on a group of halls which show evidence of design or extension for the use of two families on the 'unit system' appears in J. T. Smith, 'Lancashire and Cheshire Houses . . .', *Archaeological Journal*, Vol. 127, 1970.

f. The Two-Unit Family. Many examples of the various versions of this plan may be found in S. R. Jones and J. T. Smith, 1963 on. The term 'direct entry' has come into use to describe those two-unit houses in which the front door opens directly into the principal ground floor room without the interposition of any lobby or cross-passage.

g. The Central Fireplace Family. For a general discussion of the plan see A. Quiney, 'The Lobby-entrance House, its origins and distribution' in *Architectural History*, Vol. 27, 1984. An early example, though possibly not vernacular, is described in N. Summers, 'Old Hall Farm, Kneesall', *Transactions of the Thoroton Society*, Vol. 76, 1972. The plan-type is also described in C. A. Hewett, 'The development of the post-medieval house', *Post-Medieval Archaeology*, Vol. 7, 1973.

h. Double Pile Plans. The term 'double pile' was used by Sir Roger Pratt about 1675 for 'polite' versions of this plan (see R. T. Gunther, *The Architecture of Sir Roger Pratt*, 1928) but the term is convenient in describing vernacular houses which are two rooms deep. For a full discussion see M. W. Barley, 'The Double Pile House', *Archaeological Journal*, Vol. 136, 1979.

i. Sections. A well-illustrated example of an open hall may be seen in P. Smith and F. Lloyd, 'Plas-ucha, Llangar, Corwen', *TAMS*, Vol. 12, 1964, and of a croglofft type section in Sir Cyril Fox, 'Peasant Crofts in North Pembrokeshire', *Antiquity*, Dec. 1937. The subject is also well covered in E. Mercer, 1975 and P. Smith, 1975.

j. Staircases. Detailed drawings of various staircases of vernacular inspiration may be seen in Fox and Raglan, 1951 on, especially Vol. III. A brief historical study of staircases in one city is F. F. Johnson, *Historic Staircases in Durham City*, City of Durham Trust, 1970. See also W. J. Smith, 'the Staircase Café, Stockport', *Transactions of the Lancs. and Chesh. Antiq. Soc.*, Vol. 79, 1977.

ARCHITECTURAL DETAILS

a. Generally. Most general books and articles on individual buildings include drawings and photographs of the architectural details but particular attention is drawn to J. Ayres, 1981 and to comparative collections of such details in Fox and Raglan, 1951, P. Smith, 1975, M. Wood, 1965 and R. B. Wood-Jones, 1963. The books produced by architects and antiquaries of the early 20C. also often contain photographs and drawings of details; see, for example, Fletcher Moss, *Pilgrimages to Old Homes*.

b. Windows and Doors. C. F. Innocent, 1916, includes many interesting details. W. O. Davies and H. Tanner, *Old English Doorways*, 1903, is useful on doorways. Window surrounds of between 1674 and 1804 are illustrated in RCHM, *Inventory for Stamford*, HMSO, 1977. The development of the double-hung sash window is explained in detail by H. Louw, 'The Origin of the Sash Window', *Architectural History*, Vol. 26, 1983.

a. Generally. Recently published general surveys include the following:
Brunskill, R. W., *Traditional Farm Buildings of Britain*, Gollancz, 1982.
Harvey, N., *A History Of Farm Buildings*, David and Charles, 1970 and 1984.
Harvey, N., *The Industrial Archaeology of Farming in England and Wales*, Batsford, 1980.
Peters, J. E. C., *Discovering Traditional Farm Buildings*, Shire, 1981.
Weller, J., *History of the Farmstead: Development of Energy Sources*, Faber and Faber, 1982.
Wiliam, E., *Historical Farm Buildings of Wales*, Donald, 1986.

Regional studies completed include the comprehensive *Farm Buildings of Western Lowland Staffordshire*, Manchester University Press, 1969, and the equally comprehensive E. Wiliam, *Traditional Farm Buildings in North-East Wales*, National Museum of Wales, 1982. There is also a section on farm buildings in R. W. Brunskill, 1974. The important and well-illustrated article by C. F. Stell, 'Pennine Houses' in *Folk Life*, Vol. 3, 1965 introduced the 'laithe-house' combination of house and farm buildings.

Studies of individual farmsteads are occasionally published e.g. N. W. Alcock, 'Bury Barton, Lapford, Devon', *Transactions of the Devonshire Association*, Vol. 98, 1966.

For contemporary accounts of farm-building design, the *General Surveys* made, county by county for the Board of Agriculture at the end of the 18C. and beginning of the 19C. are sometimes useful as are the Prize Essays published in the *Journal of the Royal Agricultural Society of England* from about 1850 onwards. The designs for model farmsteads included in e.g. J. C. Loudon, *The Encyclopedia of Agriculture*, 1842, or collected in e.g. J. Bailey Denton, *The Farm Homesteads of England*, 2nd ed. 1845 are not strictly vernacular but are useful in illustrating farming practice.

b. Location and Layout. For the siting of farmsteads in relation to villages and land settlement see B. K. Roberts, 1986 and C. Taylor, 1983. Very useful also is M. W. Beresford and J. K. St. Joseph, *Medieval England: an Aerial Survey*, Cambridge University Press, 2nd ed., 1979. The combination of farmhouse and farm buildings in the longhouse form has been covered in references to two-unit houses above and in the laithe-house form in Stell, 1965.

c. Combination Arrangements. The bank barn was recognized as a building type by J. Walton in 'Upland Houses', *Antiquity*, No. 30, 1950, and described by R. W. McDowall in 'The Westmorland Vernacular' in W. A. Singleton (ed.), *Studies in Architectural History*, Vol. II, York, 1956. I recognized the American relationship and brought over the American term in the first edition of this book. For further information see R. W. Brunskill, *Traditional Farm Buildings . . .*, 1982.

d. The Barn for Hand Threshing. Many studies of individual barns have been published though they are mainly the superior barns of monastic estates. A fine collection appears in W. Horn and E. Born, *The Barns of the Abbey*

of Beaulieu at its Granges of Great Coxwell and Beaulieu St. Leonards,
University of California Press, 1965. An important early study was S. E.
Rigold, 'Some Major Kentish Barns' in *Archaeologia Cantiana*, Vol. 81,
1961. A range of individual barn studies from different parts of England
would include F. W. B. Charles and W. Horn, 'The Cruck-built Barn of
Leigh Court, Worcs.', *Journal of the Society of Architectural Historians*
(USA), Vol. 32, 1973; S. Jones, 'Gunthwaite Hall Barn, South Yorkshire',
Archaeological Journal, Vol. 137, 1980, and J. E. C. Peters, 'The Tithe Barn,
Arreton', Isle of Wight, *TAMS*, Vol. 12, 1964.

e. The Barn for Machine Threshing. For the machines around which the later
farm buildings were designed see G. E. Fussell, *The Farmers Tools*, 1952,
and M. Partridge, *Farm Tools through the Ages*, 1973. The design and
development of the horse engine is described in F. Atkinson, 'The Horse
as a source of Rotary Power', *Transactions of the Newcomen Society*, Vol. 33,
1960–1; see also S. Macdonald, 'The Progress of the Early Threshing Machine', *Agricultural History Review*, 1975 and 1978, and, for distribution of
horse engine houses, K. Hutton, 'The Distribution of Wheelhouses in the
British Isles', *Agricultural History Review*, Vol. 24, 1976

f. The Shelter Shed and Linhay. N. W. Alcock, 'Devonshire Linhays', *Transactions of the Devonshire Association*, Vol. 95, 1963, gives a thorough and
well-illustrated account of a building type since widely recognized.

g. Kilns, Oast Houses and Maltings. Useful references include A. H. Burges,
Hops, 1964 and I. Homes, 'The Agricultural Use of the Herefordshire House
and its Outbuildings', *VA*, Vol. 9, 1970. For corn-drying kilns some information appears in D. H. Jones and J. K. Major, 'Drying Kilns attached to
Corn Mills', *Conference Proceedings*, International Molinological Society,
1973, while G. Beresford, 'Three Deserted Medieval Settlements on Dartmoor', *Medieval Archaeology*, Vol. 23, 1979 gives details of kilns used in
a deteriorating climate on Dartmoor. The traditional layout of small maltings may be followed from C. J. Loudon, *An Encyclopedia of Cottage, Farm
and Villa Architecture*, and from J. Lugar, *The Country Gentleman's Architect*, 1807.

URBAN VERNACULAR, MINOR INDUSTRIAL AND OTHER VERNACULAR
BUILDINGS

a. Urban Vernacular Generally. A thorough introduction is provided by D.
Lloyd, *The Making of English Towns*, Gollancz, 1984. Background material
appears in M. Aston and J. Bond, *The Landscape of Towns*, 1976. An interesting anthology of contemporary descriptions is contained in R. C. Richardson
and T. B. James, *The Urban Experience: a Sourcebook*, Manchester University Press, 1983. Among the more recent *Inventories* of the RCHM (England)
those of Salisbury, Stamford and York contain a great deal on urban
vernacular.

b. Medieval Urban Vernacular. General studies M. W. Beresford and J. K. St.

Joseph, 1979, M. W. Beresford, *New Towns of the Middle Ages*, Lutterworth Press, 1967, C. Platt, *The English Medieval Town*, Secker, 1976. For a thorough study of a town full of medieval urban buildings see V. Parker, *The Making of King's Lynn*, Phillimore, 1971. Some new information on 16C. houses and cottages in London appears in J. Schofield, *The Building of London from the Conquest to the Great Fire*, British Museum Publications, 1984. The series on houses in Ludlow published by the Ludlow Research Group (e.g. D. Lloyd, *Broad Street*, Ludlow Research Papers No. 3, 1979) are thorough studies of individual buildings or small groups. Important articles include W. A. Pantin, 'Medieval English Town-House Plans', *Medieval Archaeology*, Vols. 6–7, 1962–3, and P. A. Faulkner, 'Medieval Undercrofts and Town Houses', *Archaeological Journal*, Vol. 123, 1966.

c. Urban Vernacular of the 17C., 18C., and early 19C. For background see C. W. Chalkin, *The Provincial Towns of Georgian England*, 1974. Useful articles include A. F. Kelsall, 'The London House Plan in the late 17th Century ' and R. F. Taylor, 'Town Houses in Taunton', both in *Post-Medieval Archaeology*, Vol. 8, 1974. S. E. Rasmussen, *London the Unique City*, Penguin, 1960, and J. Summerson, *Georgian London*, Penguin, 1962, include some vernacular material.

d. Cottage Industry and Industrial Housing. The housing conditions in the early 19C. have been amply, if sometimes partially reported in many text books of town planning. A useful summary may be seen in W. Ashworth, *The Genesis of Modern British Town Planning*, Routledge and Kegan Paul, 1954. The importance of cottage industry and early industrial housing as both a rural and an urban phenomenon may be seen from S. D. Chapman (ed.), *The History of Working Class Housing*, David and Charles, 1971, especially the chapter by W. J. Smith. The article by O. Ashmore, 'Low Moor, Clitheroe, a Nineteenth Century Factory Community', *Trans. Lancs. and Chesh. Antiq. Soc.*, Vols. 73–4, 1963–4, illustrates clearly the link between factories and cottages. R. Leech, *Early Industrial Housing : the Trinity Area of Frome*, HMSO, 1981, and W. G. Muter, *The Buildings of an Industrial Community : Coalbrookdale and Ironbridge*, Phillimore, 1979, deal with cottages in specific industrial communities as does W. Barke, 'Weavers' Cottages in the Huddersfield Area', *Folk Life*, Vol. 17, 1949. J. Lowe, *Welsh Industrial Workers' Housing*, National Museum of Wales, 1977, and S. Muthesius, *The English Terraced House*, Yale, 1982, deal with the topic more widely. Many books on regional industrial archaeology include chapters on cottage industry and industrial housing—D. M. Smith, *Industrial Archaeology of the East Midlands*, David and Charles, 1967 is a good example. See also Caffyn, 1986.

e. Minor Industrial Vernacular including Windmills and Watermills. Here the literature of industrial archaeology forms the basis. Examples include R. A. Buchanan, *Industrial Archaeology in Britain*, Penguin, 1972, and N. Cossons, *The BP Book of Industrial Archaeology*, David and Charles, 1975. For specific building types see R. T. Clough, *The Lead Smelting Mills of the Yorkshire Dales*, published by the author, 1962, L. Sysons, *British Water*

Mills, Batsford, 1965, R. Wailes, *Windmills in England*, Architectural Press, 1948, and J. Reynolds, *Windmills and Watermills*, Hugh Evelyn, 1970.

f. Other Vernacular Buildings. The early nonconformist meeting houses were unobtrusive in design and clearly related to traditional domestic buildings in many ways. See H. G. Arnold, 'Early Meeting Houses', *TAMS*, Vol. 8, 1960. The first of an authoritative series on chapels prepared by C. F. Stell for the RCHM (England) will be *An Inventory of Nonconformist Chapels and Meeting Houses in Central England*, HMSO, 1987. Village schools also may be vernacular buildings and a well-developed example is described and illustrated in B. C. Redwood, 'Audlem Free Grammar School', *Journal of the Chester and North Wales Architectural, Archaeological and Historic Society*, Vol. 51, 1964.

COMPARISONS AND CONCLUSIONS

a. Distribution Maps and Time Scales. The maps of walling and roofing materials used in part of Cumberland are based on R. W. Brunskill, 'Traditional Domestic Architecture of the Eden Valley' and 'Traditional Domestic Architecture of the Solway Plain', unpublished theses, University of Manchester, 1952 and 1963 respectively. The map of building regions is based on that in P. Smith, 'The Architectural Personality of the British Isles', *Archaeologia Cambrensis*, Vol. 129, 1980. Similar but dot-type distribution maps and similar time-scales may be found in other unpublished theses, University of Manchester: M. E. Little, 'Traditional Domestic Architecture in Parts of Shropshire'; T. L. Marsden, 'Traditional Domestic Architecture in the Lower Trent Valley', and 'Traditional Domestic Architecture in Rutland'; D. V. McCaig, 'Traditional Domestic Architecture in Cheshire'; J. E. Partington, 'Traditional Domestic Architecture of North Lancashire'; R. S. Partington, 'Traditional Domestic Architecture of South Lancashire'; W. A. Singleton, 'Traditional Domestic Architecture in parts of Cheshire and Derbyshire'; P. Tolhurst, 'The Vernacular Architecture of Norfolk, a Sample Survey': G. L. Worsley, 'Traditional Domestic Architecture in the Cotswolds'.

National distribution maps appear in R. W. Brunskill, 'Distribution of Building Materials etc.', *TAMS*, Vol. 23, 1978, and in P. Smith, 1980. Regional maps appear in J. and J. Penoyre, 1978. There are several distribution maps in L. Hall, 1983, and in B. Harrison and B. Hutton, 1984, and many in P. Smith, 1975.

For interpretation of evidence from inscribed dates see B. Hutton, 'Rebuilding in Yorkshire: the Evidence of Inscribed Dates', *VA*, Vol. 8, 1977.

b. Vernacular Architecture and North America. Publication of books on the relationship between vernacular architecture in Britain and North America has reflected the various phases of the study. One phase is represented by such books as J. F. Kelly, *Early Domestic Architecture of Connecticut*, 1924, Dover edition 1963, and F. Kimball, *Domestic Architecture of the American Colonies and of the Early Republic*, 1922, Dover edition, 1966, and, a little later, H. C. Forman, *The Architecture of the Old South*, Harvard University Press, 1948. The phase was summarized in H. Morrison, *Early American Architecture*, Oxford University Press (New York), 1952. An early book devoted to links between the vernacular architecture of both sides of the Atlantic is M. S. Briggs, *Homes of the Pilgrim Fathers in England and America 1620–1685*, Oxford University Press (New York). 1932. The academic approach to the subject was superbly maintained in A. L. Cummings, *The Framed Houses of Massachusetts Bay: 1625–1725*, Belknap Press, 1979. A new phase and a different approach to the subject was introduced by H. Glassie in *Pattern in the Material Folk Culture of the Eastern United States*, University of Pennsylvania Press, 1969 (with a bibliography 73 pages long), and developed in H. Glassie, *Folk Housing in Middle Virginia, Knoxville, Tennessee*, 1975. A third phase is marked by a vast expansion of interest in vernacular architecture in the USA and Canada, much of it devoted to aspects unrelated to British precedent, and the flood of books and articles has produced a published bibliography, H. W. Marshall, *American Folk Architecture: A Selected Bibliography*, Library of Congress, Washington DC, 1981 and the ever-expanding bibliographies prepared by D. Upton in the *Bulletins* of the Vernacular Architecture Forum (USA). D. Upton and J. Vlach have edited an anthology *Common Places, Readings in American Vernacular Architecture*, University of Georgia Press, 1985. A further dimension has been added by C. Carson and others, 'Impermanent Architecture in the Southern American Colonies', *Winterthur Portfolio*, 16, Nos 2/3, 1981, showing that in Maryland and Virginia at least, colonists erected first their temporary tents or 'English wigwams', then impermanent earth-fast post structures were used for several years before resources and adequate security allowed conventional permanent timber-framed houses to be erected. Other scholars who have published material linking British and American vernacular architecture include Candee, Hart and Mather.

c. A Note on Vernacular Architecture in Scotland. For the rural setting see R. N. Millman, *The Making of the Scottish Landscape*, Batsford, 1975. For the setting of urban vernacular buildings see C. McWilliam, *Scottish Townscapes*, Collins, 1975. For the architectural context see J. G. Dunbar, *The Historic Architecture of Scotland*, Batsford, 1966. The various county *Inventories* of the Royal Commission on the Ancient Monuments of Scotland, especially the more recent, include works of vernacular as well as polite architecture. Two important comprehensive works have been published recently: A. Fenton and B. Walker, *The Rural Architecture of Scotland*, Donald, 1981 (which related traditional buildings, especially farm buildings to their social and economic setting) and R. Naismith, *Buildings of the Scottish Countryside*, Gollancz, 1985. The latter summarizes the conclusions from a survey of the external appearance of Scottish rural houses based on a sample of 23,000 examples and culminates in the definition of architectural character zones. There are also many articles now in print including those in the annual *Newsletter* of the Scottish Vernacular Building Working Group and those in the *Journal* of the School for Scottish Studies of Edinburgh University.

d. A Note on Vernacular Architecture in Ireland. There is no single work on the subject but introductory material was included in E. E. Evans, *Irish Folk Ways*, Routledge and Kegan Paul, 1957. The northern part of the island (not solely Northern Ireland) has been admirably covered by A. Gailey in *Rural Housing of the North of Ireland*, Donald, 1984 including sections devoted to British influence where found. The close relationship between folk life and building form is described in H. Glassie, *Passing the Time*, O'Brien, Dublin, 1982. For Ireland generally there is an excellent brief account in *Ireland's Vernacular Architecture*, Mercier Press, Dublin, 1975, by C. O'Danachair (K. Danaher) who has also published *A Bibliography of Irish Ethnology and Folk Tradition*, Mercier Press, Dublin, 1978.

e. The Vernacular Revival. The reference to Petit is taken from P. Collins, *Changing Ideals in Modern Architecture*, Faber and Faber, 1965, p. 122; Collins devoted pp.173–84 to 'Linguistic Analogy'. For an account of the work of Edgar Wood see J. H. G. Archer, 'Edgar Wood, a Notable Manchester Architect', *Trans. Lancs. and Chesh. Antiq. Soc.*, Vols. 73–4, 1963–4.

APPENDIX I: HOW TO STUDY VERNACULAR ARCHITECTURE

a. Generally. Study depends on both fieldwork and library or archive work. While the study can certainly be done individually many beginners find it helpful to join one of the existing study groups. Affiliated to the Vernacular Architecture Group are such study groups as that of the Avoncroft Museum of Building, Bromsgrove, Warwickshire; the Bedfordshire, Buckinghamshire and Cambridgeshire Group; the Domestic Buildings Research Group (Surrey); the Essex Architectural Research Society; the Herefordshire Extra-Mural Research Group; the North Yorkshire and Cleveland Vernacular Buildings Study Group; the Petersfield Area Historical Society; the Sevenoaks District Architectural History Group; the South Avon Vernacular Buildings Research Group; the Suffolk Buildings Research Group; the Wealden Buildings Research Group; the Wiltshire Buildings Record; and the Yorkshire Archaeological Society. Because of frequent changes it is not practicable to give addresses here but local libraries or record offices usually know of such groups. A useful introduction to fieldwork is R. W. McDowall, *Recording Old Houses: a Guide*, Council for British Archaeology, 1980. Four levels of survey are distinguished: a. superficial, external only; b. superficial, external and internal; c. measured; d. destructive.

b. Extensive Recording. The Manchester method was briefly described by R. A. Cordingley, 1948. It has been thoroughly described and illustrated in R. W. Brunskill, 'A Systematic Procedure for Recording English Vernacular Architecture', *TAMS*, Vol. 13, 1965–6 (offprints are available from the Ancient Monuments Society). It represents level a. in McDowall, 1980 above as does the simplified version described and illustrated here. For a development designed to cover the recording of farm buildings see R. W. Brunskill, 'Recording the Buildings of the Farmstead', *TAMS*, Vol. 21, 1975–6 (offprints also available from the Society); This represents level b. in the list above.

248

c. Intensive Recording. Measuring and drawing techniques have been described in various books on draughtsmanship for architectural students. R.
Fraser Reekie, *Draughtsmanship*, Arnold, 1969, is one of the best known.
J. K. Major, *Fieldwork in Industrial Archaeology*, Batsford, 1975, is an excellent practical guide to measuring vernacular buildings as well as the mounu-
ments of industrial archaeology. R. Chitham, *Measured Drawing for
Architects*, Architectural Press, 1980, is a thorough guide to measuring and
drawing techniques for works of vernacular and polite architecture. T.
Buchanan, *Photographing Historic Buildings*, HMSO, 1983, is very useful.

d. Documentary Investigation. W. G. Hoskins, *Local History in England*,
explains sources and techniques appropriate to this sort of investigation.
J. H. Harvey, *Sources for the History of Houses*, British Records Association,
1974, is written by another expert. Also useful is D. Iredale, *Enjoying Archives*, David and Charles, 1973.

e. Destructive Recording. When, sadly, vernacular buildings have to be taken
down there is a wonderful opportunity to record to a depth not possible
in studying an existing building. One can record masonry techniques, timber
jointing, details of plaster craftsmanship etc. The article by E. Wiliam, 'A
Cruck Barn at Hendre Wen, Llanrwst, Denbighshire', *TAMS*, Vol. 21,
1976, relates the discoveries made when a barn was dismantled prior to re-
erection at the Welsh Folk Museum.

f. Accessible Vernacular Buildings. See J. R. Armstrong, *Traditional Buildings Accessible to the Public*, E. P. Publications, 1979.

INDEX

Aberdeen bond, 209
Addy, S. O., 18, 232
Aisled barns, 78–9, 151
Aisled hall plans, 78–9, 103, 114, 241
Aisle post, 78–9
Alcock, N., 111, 186, 234, 239
Almondbury, Yorks, 226
American vernacular architecture, 64, 68, 200–5, 246–7
Arcade plate, 78–9
Arch braces, 80–1
Arched doorways, 132–3, 136
Armstrong, J. R., 249
Ashlar (masonry), 40–1
Ashlaring (roof construction), 77
Ashworth, W., 245
Aston, M., 244
Ayres, J., 232

Back-to-back fireplaces, 107, 168
Back-to-back houses and cottages, 176, 178–9
Baffle entry plans, 106–7
Baillie-Scott, M. H., 211
Balanced sash windows, 131
Balloon framing, 54, 201
Barge boards, 75, 97, 139, 230
Barley, M. W., 228, 232
Barns, 24, 143, 148–53, 161, 229, 230
  bank barns, 148–9, 229, 243
  hand threshing barns, 143, 150–1
  hay barns, 144, 161, 229
  machine threshing barns, 152–3, 244
Bastel houses, 100–1, 241
Bath, 170
Batsford, H., 232
Beresford, M. W., 243, 244
Bay windows, 138–9
Bibliographies, 232
Billet, M., 240
Blackhouses, 207–8
Blades (cruck and related construction), 55, 82–3
Bond, J., 244
Bonnet hip tiles, 91
Born, E., 243
Bow windows, 138–9
Box-frame construction, 34, 54–5, 80–1, 202–3

Breconshire, 230
Brick arches, 48–9
Brick nogging, 70–1, 238
Brick taxes, 46, 62
Brick ties, 49
Brick tile cladding, 62–3
Brick walling , 46–9, 184, 189, 210, 238
Bridgwater, 92
Briggs, M. S., 232, 247
Brunskill, R. W., 228, 232, 233, 238, 239, 240, 243
Buchanan, R. A., 245
Buchanan, T., 249
Building accounts, 225
Butt-edged weatherboard, 65
Buttery, position on plan, 102–3, 106–7, 115
Butt purlin roofs, 72, 80–1

Caernarvonshire, 176
Caffyn, L., 233
Cambridgeshire, 50, 102, 201
Cart sheds, 144, 158–9, 229–30
Cast-iron cladding, 68–9
Cavetto mould mullions, 127
Cellars, 117, 167
Central fireplace plans, 106–7, 118, 242
Central service room plans, 108–9
Chalklin, C. W., 245
Chapman, S. D., 245
Charles, F. W. B., 57, 239
Chesher, V. M. and F. J., 233
Cheshire, 57, 88, 161
Chimney pots, 94–5
Chimneys, 94–5, 204–5
Chitham, R., 249
Clapboarding (weatherboarding), 64–5, 202
Classification of plans, 99–113
Clay etc., walling, 50–1, 184, 190, 238
Clifton-Taylor, A., 232, 238
Clipsham, 88
Clough, R. T., 245
Cobble walling, 36, 42–3, 62, 188
Cochwillan, 180–1
Collar purlins, 76–7
Collar rafter roofs, 75, 116
Collars, 80–1
Common rafters, 80–3, 85, 89, 91, 93

Conway, 166
Cordingley, R. A., 15, 186, 214, 228, 236, 241
Corn drying kilns, 145, 163, 181, 244
Corn in agriculture, 143–4
Cornwall, 27, 86
Cossons, N., 245
Cotswolds, 88, 195
Cottages, 22–4, 166, 176–7, 186, 199, 202, 210, 215
Cottage industry, building for, 160–3, 245
'Courtyard' farmstead layout, 147
Cow houses, 154–5, 229, 230
'Croglofft' cottages, 115, 120, 176
Cross-passage plans, 97–107, 115, 197
Cruck construction, 35, 54–5, 82–3, 186, 191, 239
    base crucks, 80–1
    cruck blades, 55, 82–3
    cruck spurs, 82–3
    cruck ties, 82–3
    cruck trusses in open halls, 103
    jointed crucks, 191
Cumberland, 27, 100, 180
Cummings, A. L., 247

Danaher, K., 248
Davies, W. O., 242
Dearne's bond, 49
Decorated lintels, 134–5
Denmark, 148
Dentilation, 49
Denton, J. Bailey, 243
Devon, 86, 111, 176
Diamond mullions, 127
Diaper work, 47
Documentary investigation, 214–27
Dogleg stairs, 120–1
Dogtooth ornament, 49
Doors and doorways, 125, 132–7, 199, 230
    medieval phase, 132–3
    renaissance phase, 136–7
    sub-medieval phase, 134–5
Dormer windows, 96–7, 114, 116–17, 230
Double-ended hall plans, 102–3
Double fronted houses, 112–13
Double hung sash windows (balanced sashes), 123, 130–1
Double pile plans, 75, 112–13, 120, 205, 242
Double roof, 72, 76–7

Dovecots, 152
Drip moulds (label moulds), 126–7, 130, 132–3
Drystone walling, 38
Dunbar, J. G., 247
Durham, 180
Dutch barns, 161
Dutch gables, 75, 97

Earth etc, walling, 50–1, 232
East Anglia, 44, 64, 176, 180, 190, 202
Eastern counties of England, 46, 54, 57, 90, 92, 112, 201, 204
Eaves details, 75, 97, 207, 230
Eden, P., 241
English bond brickwork, 47
Evans, E. E., 248
Extensive recording, 214–19, 248
Exwood, M., 240
'Eyebrow' dormers, 96–7

Farm buildings, 24, 142–62, 228–9, 243–4
Farmstead layouts, 146–7
    locations, 147, 243
Farmyards, 146–7, 160
Feather-edged weatherboarding, 65
Feeding passages, 155
Fenton, A., 247
Field barns (field houses), 144, 161, 229
Fiennes, Celia, 225
Filtering-down process, 176
Fireplace positions, 99–115, 118–19, 175, 202–3
First floor hall plans, 100–1, 241
Fishscale pattern tiles, 61, 91
Flags, see Stone flag roofing
Flint walling, 44–5, 188
Forman, H. C., 247
Fox, C., 233
Fry, C., 232
Fussell, G. E., 244
Fylde (Lancashire), 180

Gable details, 75
Gabled roofs, 75
Gailey A., 238, 248
Galleries, 204–5
Galletting, 39, 93
Gambrel roof, 74–5, 116, 203
Garrets, 114, 117
Garretting, see Galletting
Gauged brickwork, 46–7, 130
Gee, E. A., 239

251

Germany, 148
Giles, C., 233
Glass and glazing, 123, 131
Glassie, H., 241, 247, 248
Gothic Revival details, 131
Granaries, 144–5, 156, 158–9, 229–30
Great Coxwell (Berks), 142
Great Houses, 22
Great Rebuilding, 27, 201, 237
Grid-iron development, 166
Gunther, R. T., 242

Hall, L., 233
Hall plans, 102–3, 241, see also First
    floor hall plans
Hamlets, 146–7
Hammer beam roof construction, 80–1
Hand-loom weavers, 172–5
Harding, J. M., 234
Harr-hung doors, 125, 133
Harris, R., 238
Harrison, B., 234
Harrison, William, 225
Harvey, J. H., 249
Harvey, N., 243
Hathern (Leics), 173
Header bond brickwork, 47
Hearth position (see also Fireplaces), 99–
    115, 119, 173
Herefordshire, 59
Herring-bone brick infill, 71
Hewett, C. A., 239
Highland regions, 185, 246
Hipped roofs and hip details, 74, 86, 89,
    91
Historic American Buildings Survey,
    201
Hooded chimney (smoke hood), 115,
    119
Horizontally sliding sash windows
    (Yorkshire sliding sash), 123, 128–9
Horn, W., 243
Horse engines, 152–3, 180, 229, 244
Hoskins, W. G., 232, 235, 237
Hutton, B., 234

Industrial housing, 176–9, 245
Industrial vernacular architecture, 20,
    24, 180–3, 244–6
Innocent, C. F., 18, 232, 242
Inside cross-passage plans, 108–9, 111
Intensive surveys (measured drawings),
    220-2
Iredale, D., 249

Ireland, 247–8
Ireson, A. S., 238, 240
Isle of Man, 26, 86

James, T. B., 244
Jamestown, Virginia, 204
Jettied timber walling, 56–7, 102, 167,
    203
Jointed crucks, see Cruck construction
Jones, S. R., 233
Jones, S. R. (Stanley), 234
Jowls, 79

Keeping holes, 156
Kelly, J. F., 246
Kendal (Westmorland), 68
Kent, 27, 163, 193, 210
Kentish Rag walling, 38
Kerridge (Cheshire), 88
Kilns, 163, 244
    limekilns, 182–3
    pottery kilns, 182–3
Kimball, F., 246
King mullion, 127
King post roof construction, 83
King's Lynn, 166
Kitchen positions, 102–3, 112–13, 115,
    174–5, 177, 226–7
Kneeler detail, 75

Label moulds, 126–7, 130–1, 134–5
Laced valley, 89, 96
Lacey, H. M. and U. E., 235
Lacing courses, 43
Ladder access to upper floors, 100–1,
    115, 120–1, 175
Laithe houses, 147, 243
Lake District, 37, 68, 85, 88, 94, 134,
    148, 163, 211
Lancashire, 58, 68–9, 123, 161, 176, 225
Lancet windows, 127
Lapped weatherboarding, 65
Large Houses, 22, 24, 186, 199, 202, 215
Lead cames, 127
Ledge and plank doors, 132–3
Leech, R., 245
Leeds, 176
Leicestershire, 86
Lethaby, W. R., 211
Lincolnshire, 68–9
Linhay, 144, 160, 244
Lloyd, D., 244
Lloyd, N., 233, 238

Lobby entrance plans (central fireplaces), 106–7, 118
London, 46, 92, 170
Longhouse plans, 104–5, 111, 143, 147, 243
Loudon, J. C., 243, 244
Louvres, 115
Lowe, J., 234, 245
'Lower' end of a house, 99
Lowland regions, 185
L-shaped farmstead layout, 147
Lugar, J., 244
Lutterworth (Leics), 70
Lutyens, Sir Edwin, 211

McCann, J., 238
Macclesfield (Cheshire), 175
McDowall, R. W., 243, 248
Machin, R., 235, 237
Mackay, W. B., 238
McLintock, M. E., 235
McWilliam, C., 247
Magpie work, 66
Major, J. K., 249
Maltings, 163, 244
Manchester, University of, 214
Mansard roofs, 74–5
Marsden, T. L., 57
Marshall, H. W., 247
Martin, D., 235
Mason, R. T., 234
Mass walling, 35, 37–51
Mastin, B., 235
Mathematical tile cladding, 62–3, 193, 240
Measured drawings, 220–32, 249
Mechanical tile cladding, see Mathematical tile cladding
Meikle, Andrew, 152
Mercer, E., 233
Midland Counties, 47, 54, 58, 66, 161, 172, 186
Millman, R. N., 247
Monmouthshire, 186
Morris, William, 211
Morrison, H., 247
Moss, F., 242
Moulded bricks, 46–7
Mouldings, 125–37, 141
  on ceiling beams, 141
  on doorways, 132
  on panelling, 141
  on window jambs and mullions, 126–31, 186, 199

M-shaped roof, 74–5
Mud and stud walling, 68
Mullioned windows, 124, 126–9, 131, 173, 175, 211, 212–13
Multi-storey sections, 117
Muntin and plank partitions, 140–1
Muter, W. G., 245
Muthesius, S., 245

Naismith, R., 247
National Monuments Records, 236
National Trust, 19
Nevill, R., 234
Newel staircases, 120–1
New England, 106, 201, 203–4
Norfolk, 43, 51, 84–5, 211
Normal assembly, 78–9
Northern Counties of England, 27, 47, 54, 57, 66, 115, 130, 143, 186
Northumberland, 100, 176, 180
North Wales, 68, 176, 180

Oast houses, 144–5, 163
O'Danachair, C., 248
Ogee arched windows, 127
Oldham (Lancashire), 172
Oliver, P., 235
One and a half storey sections, 116, 178
Open halls, 102–3, 118–19
  in plan, 102–3
  in section, 114–15, 140
Open hearth, 115, 118–19, 168, see also Hearths and Fireplaces
Oriel windows, 138–9
Outshuts, 99, 107, 113, 117, 202
Ovolo moulded mullions, 127
Oxen, use and accommodation, 143, 154–5
Oxfordshire, 186

Palladian windows, 130–1
Panelled doors, 136–7
Panelling, 140–1
Pantile roofing, 92–3, 96, 196
Pantry, position on plan, 102–3, 105, 107, 112
Parallel farmstead layout, 147
Parapet details, 75, 85
Pargetting, 66–7
Parker, V., 245
Parlour, position on plan, 99, 105, 107, 108, 110–11
Partridge, M., 244
Partitions, 140–1

Passing brace, 78–9
Pearson, S., 234
Peate, I. C., 18, 233
Pebble walling, 42–3, 188
Pembroke, 94, 111
Pennant, William, 225
Pennines, 37, 38, 88, 172, 176, 187, 195
Pennsylvania, 148, 200, 201
Penoyre, J. and J., 233
Peters, J. E. C., 228, 240
Petit, J. L., 211
Pig-sties, 145, 162, 229
Pitching eyes, 157, 229
Plain-tile cladding, 60–1, 193
Plain-tile roofing, 74, 90–1, 96, 196, 197
Plan forms, 99–113, 240–2
    central fireplace plans, 106–7, 198,
        242
    central service room plans, 108–9
    double pile plans, 112–13, 242
    first floor plans, 100–1, 241
    hall plans, 102–3, 241
    inside cross-passage plans, 108–9
    side wall fireplace plans, 110–11, 197
    two-unit plans, 104–5, 242
Planning theory, 241
Plaster cladding, 66–7, 193
Platform framing, 54
Platt, C., 245
Polite threshold, 25, 29
Porches, 138–9, 204–5
Post mills, 181
Potter, M. and A., 233
Principal rafters, 81
Prior, E. S., 211
Prizeman, J., 233
Probate inventories, 225–8
Purlins, 72, 80–3, 116, 117

Quoins, 39, 41

Rafter roofs, 72
Raglan, Lord, 233
Railways, effects of, 86
Rainwater heads, 75, 139
Raised crucks, 83
Raised eaves, 114, 116
Ramm, H. G., 241
Rapaport, A., 235
Rasmussen, S. E., 245
Rat trap bond, 48–9
Reekie, R. Fraser, 249
Regency, 138
Reversed assembly, 78–9

Reynolds, J., 246
Richardson, R. C., 244
Ridge, details at, 85, 87, 89, 91
Roberts, B. K., 235
Rochdale (Lancashire), 212
Roof construction, 72–83, 240
Roof lights, 96–7, 117
Room names, 228
Row housing (terrace housing), 170–1,
    174–5
Royal Commissions on Historical
    Monuments, 18, 234
Rubble masonry, 38–9
Rudofsky, B., 235
Rutland, 88
Ryder, P. F., 239

St. Albans (Herts), 166
St. Joseph, J. K., 243
Salisbury (Wilts), 166
Saltbox section (U.S.A.), 206–7
Salzman, L. F., 233
Sandon, E., 234
Scarf joints, 78–9
Scattered farmstead layout, 147
Schofield, J., 245
Scotland, 206–9, 247
Scottish border, 92, 100
Screens, passage, 102, 115
Sectional form, 114–17, 230
Shaw, R. Norman, 211
Sheffield, 176
Shelter sheds, 144, 160, 229, 244
Shropshire, 59
Side hung casement windows, 128–9,
    130–1
Side wall fireplaces, 110, 198
Single-ended hall plans, 102–3
Single-fronted houses or cottages,
    112–13
Single roofs, 72, 76–7
Sink mow, 161
Size-type differentiation, 22, 24, 215,
    236
Slate cladding, 68–9
Slate infill to timber walling, 71
Slate roofing, 86–7, 96, 184, 199, 210,
    230
Small Houses, 22, 24, 186, 187, 202, 215
Smith, D. M., 245
Smith, J. T., 57, 234, 239
Smith, P., 233
Smithies, 182–3
Smock mills, 181

Smoke bay, 118–19
Smoke blackening, 118–19
Smoke hood, *see* Hooded chimney
Snecked masonry walling, 39
Solar position, 103
Solway Plain, 184
Somerset, 92
Southampton, 166
South Eastern Counties, 54, 60, 62, 64, 90, 144, 176, 200, 202, 204
South Western Counties, 54, 68, 132, 133, 135, 186–7
Spere (speer), 115, 117
Spice cupboard, 140–1
Spinning gallery, 29
Splayed mullions, 137
Sprocketted eaves, 81
Stables, 144–5, 156–7, 229
Staddle stones, 159
Staffordshire, 161
Staircases, 120–1, 173, 175, 230, 242
Stell, C. F., 246
Stone flag roofing, 88–9, 96, 184, 195, 199, 240
Stone infill to timber walling, 71
Stone tile roofing, 88–9, 96, 184, 195, 199, 240
Stone walling, 37–45, 187
    distribution, 184, 187
    irregular types, 37–9, 230, 238
    regular types, 40–1
Stub tenon, 83
Suffolk, 51
Summerson, J., 245
Sussex, 27, 43, 163
Sway braces (wind braces), 82–3
Swept valley, 89, 96
Switzerland, 148
Sysons, L., 245

Tanner, H., 242
Taylor, C., 235
Terraced housing, 169, 170–1, 174–9, 245
Terriers, 224
Textile mills, 183
Thatch, 73, 84–5, 89, 94, 96, 97, 184, 194, 199, 211, 240
Thirsk, J., 233
Threshing by hand (and its effects), 84, 152–3
Threshing floor, 149, 153, 229
Threshing machines (and their effects), 84, 152–3, 244

Through or bonding stones, 37
Through purlin roof, 72, 82–3
Tie beams, 76–83
Tie plates, 49
Tie rods, 49
Tiles, *see* Plain-tile cladding, Plain-tile roofing, Stone-tile roofing
Timber frame construction, 52–3, 202–3, 204, 238–9
Timber walling, 56–7, 186, 192, 240
Tithe maps, 224–5
Title deeds, 224
Torching, 88, 92–3
Tower houses, 100–1, 241
Transomed windows, 126–7, 212–13
Traphouses, 229
Tuck pointing, 47
Tumbling-in (brickwork), 75, 95
Tunnel-back houses, 112–13
Turf walling, 50–1, 207, 238
Two-unit plans, 104–5, 198, 242
'Two up and two down' cottages, 175, 176–7

Upper crucks, 83, 116
'Upper' end of a house, 99, 115
Upper floor hall houses, *see* First floor hall plans
Upton, D., 247
U-shaped farmstead layout, 147

Valley details, 88–90
Verge, detail at, 75, 230
Vernacular Architecture Group, 15, 232, 235, 248
Vernacular Revival, 138, 210–13, 248
Vernacular threshold, 26–9
Vernacular zone, 28, 29, 236–7
Vertical boarding, 64–5
Vertically sliding sash windows, *see* Double hung sash windows
Village plans, 146–7
Virginia, 204–5
Vitrified headers, 47
Vlach, J., 247
Voysey, C. F. A., 211

Wade, J., 235
Wailes, R., 246
Wales, 26, 27, 34, 46, 100, 120, 132, 142, 143, 145, 146, 185, 186
Walker, B., 247
Walton, J., 234
Water mills, 24, 180, 245–6

Watershot stone walling, 37, 238
Water tabling, 95, 230
Watson, R. C., 235
Wattle and daub infilling, 58–9, 202
Weald, the, 187, 195
Wealden plan, 102–3, 118
Weatherboard cladding, 64–5, 160, 193, 202
Webb, Philip, 211
Weller, J., 243
West of England, *see* South Western Counties
Westmorland, 68
West Riding of Yorkshire, 102
Whalley (Lancashire), 225
Whitehaven (Cumberland), 158, 170
Whittaker, Rev T. D., 225
Wight, J. A., 238
Wiliam, E., 243
Williams-Ellis, C., 238
Winchelsea (Sussex), 166
Wind braces, *see* Sway braces
Windmills, 24, 180–1, 245–6

Windows, 124–31, 186
    medieval phase, 126–7
    renaissance phase, 130–1
    sub-medieval phase, 128–9
Window shutters (sliding and hinged), 126–7
Winnowing doors, 149, 153
Winston Magna (Leics), 175
Wood, Edgar, 211–12
Wood, M. E., 233
Woodforde, J., 238
Wood-Jones, R. B., 16, 234
Wood-mullioned windows, 126–7
Worcestershire, 210
Wordsworth, William, 225
Wrestler slate ridges, 87

Yeomans, D. T., 240
Yorkshire Dales, 125
Yorkshire Pennines, 176
Yorshire sliding sash windows, *see* Horizontally sliding sash
Young, Arthur, 225